D1436071

QUICK AFTER-WORK

Indian

vegetarian

COOKBOOK

QUICK AFTER-WORK

Indian

vegetarian

COOKBOOK

KUMUD SHAH

PIATKUS

To my children
Lavina and Kunal,
with love

Copyright © 1997 Kumud Shah

First published in 1997 by
Judy Piatkus (Publishers) Ltd
5 Windmill Street, London W1P 1HF

The moral right of the author has been asserted
*A catalogue record for this book is available from
the British Library*

ISBN 0-7499-1701-6

Designed by Paul Saunders
Illustrations by Paul Saunders
Photographs by Steve Baxter
Home economy by Meg Jansz
Styling by Marian Price

Typeset by Create Publishing Services Ltd
Printed and bound in Great Britain by
Bookcraft Ltd, Midsomer Norton, Somerset

CONTENTS

❈

ACKNOWLEDGEMENTS page vi

INTRODUCTION page 1

SPICES page 6

1. STARTERS AND SNACKS page 11

2. POTATO DISHES page 27

3. VEGETABLE DISHES page 41

4. PULSES page 59

5. RICE DISHES page 69

6. BREADS page 81

7. CHUTNEYS, RELISHES & DIPS page 91

8. SWEETS & DRINKS page 104

MENU SUGGESTIONS page 117

INDEX page 120

ACKNOWLEDGEMENTS

FIRST, my respects to my late father, Premchand Shah, and my maternal grandfather, Mr Premchand Chandaria, who both had the foresight to send me to study in England and had faith in my thirst for knowledge.

My special thanks to a very special friend, Barbara Dulley. Her constant encouragement, enthusiasm and help in reading the recipes and her humorous approach made it possible to get on with this book. I am also grateful to Barbara's sister and their friends, and all the other students who have attended my classes; they have been a source of strength and inspiration.

My heartfelt gratitude to Bhupendra Kansagra and the family for their assistance and moral guidance throughout this venture. His constructive comments on this book have been very useful.

I am grateful to my publisher Judy Piatkus, and the food editor, Heather Rocklin, for giving me the opportunity to write this book. Heather's clear thoughts and ideas have been appreciated. Also many thanks to Kelly Davis for her editorial help and resourceful suggestions.

My heartfelt thanks to my mother, Kasturben, whose wise and 'Godly' words kept up my spirits.

I have been lucky to be born into a family which is filled with talented and successful ladies, my main influences being my aunts, Manjumasi Shah (London), Sushimasi Thakker (Bombay), Aruna Chandaria (Nairobi), and my sisters-in-law, Shashi Shah (London) and Susha Shah (Ahmedabad), and my loving sisters, Lalita Shah (London) and Shaila Shah (Nairobi).

My devoted friends, Indu Shah Saroj Shah, Meena Shah, Sakina Suterwalla, Sunderben Bedi and many other friends have given me their good wishes, concern and blessings. Their flair for preparing good food has greatly influenced my own cooking and entertaining. I owe them the greatest respect.

Finally, I wish to acknowledge my husband Kishore's very valuable moral support, my daughter Lavina's enthusiasm and my son Kunal's devotion in typing the recipes in spite of all his homework. If it was not for them, my dream would not have become a reality. Kunal's love of vegetarian food is my greatest inspiration.

INTRODUCTION

THE SEED for this book was planted in my kitchen. When I started giving cookery classes, teaching English friends how to use spices and oriental vegetables, they would come to my first session enthusiastically but soon look at me in bewilderment – so many spices, so many exotic vegetables.

As the classes progressed, the cloud of amazement vanished and they all became terrific at improvising and cooking Indian vegetarian dishes.

At the end of the course they always asked, 'Why haven't you written a book?' If they could master my technique so quickly, I felt that others could easily follow my style of cooking. And so I started to collect together the recipes you see in this book.

I have been in this country for over 30 years, but I have always retained my love and enthusiasm for Indian cooking. At university in the sixties, living on a student's budget and always short of time, I became skilled at improvising with traditional Indian recipes, mixing and matching whatever was available. Each meal was a feast, even though it consisted of only one or two dishes. No grain of rice was wasted; the bottoms of the saucepans were literally licked! Of course at that time I had no idea that I was paving the path to my future career. My Biological Science degree was helpful in understanding the nutritional value of food, but the real joy lay in cooking and feeding friends.

The recipes I have chosen for this book are all straightforward, with no complicated ingredients. In most cases I have given a short introduction, with my personal tips for the dish.

I hope you will use these recipes at least some of the time, if not every day of the week. Why not introduce these flavoursome vegetable dishes as an alternative to traditional bland Western-style boiled or steamed vegetables? Variety is the key to a balanced diet.

These days, the most significant change in our diet has been the growth in demand for convenience foods. I believe my simple recipes will take less time and money and leave you with a nourishing meal and a sense of pride in eating food that is not processed or fortified with additives.

I hope you will gain inspiration from this book and use the recipes to give pleasure to your family and friends.

My motto is:

COOK WITH FLAIR
COOK WITH JOY
COOK WITH LOVE

If you start with these ingredients, which you will not find in any spice tin but within yourself, you will already be well on your way to preparing a successful meal.

INGREDIENTS

All my recipes are very simple but there are a few tips that are worth remembering when it comes to using some of the basic ingredients.

CHILLIES

The fresh green chillies mentioned in the recipes are the long cayenne variety. They keep well in the fridge. If you prefer less heat in your curries, discard the top quarter of the chilli and de-seed before using. Likewise, when using chilli powder, simply reduce the quantity for a milder flavour.

COCONUT

It only takes a few minutes to open a fresh coconut. First hammer it gently all over, then lay it down on a stone surface in the garden. If you hammer one end, it should split open. Drain the water into a container and use a butter knife to prise the flesh away from the shell. Then, using a sharp knife, peel the hard brown skin away from the white flesh. Chop the flesh finely in a food processor or grate it on the large blades of a hand grater. Grated coconut freezes very well.

Use finely desiccated coconut, available at all major supermarkets, as a garnish when fresh coconut is not handy.

Tinned coconut milk is more convenient for cooking, as no preparation is needed, but some brands are not very concentrated and lack taste. Try to use a good flavoursome tinned coconut milk.

Also now widely available is coconut cream, sold in small cartons or packets. The smooth, rich cream has all the natural flavour of fresh coconut milk; it is thick and concentrated. I prefer it to tinned coconut milk.

CORIANDER CHUTNEY

Coriander Chutney (p. 92) can be frozen in ice cube trays. Simply store the frozen cubes in a plastic box in the freezer and defrost before use.

FENUGREEK

Fresh fenugreek (also known as methi) is a small-leafed spinach-type plant which has a slightly bitter flavour and is sold in bunches like coriander. Use only the leaves because the stalks can be very hard. Pick the leaves off the stalks and use immediately or keep them in the fridge for a few days (see Fresh Herbs, below).

FRESH HERBS

Fresh curry leaves, coriander and fenugreek all keep well in the fridge for several days. Cut the roots of the coriander and fenugreek but keep the stalks intact and wrap the leaves in kitchen paper or in a brown paper bag. Only wash when ready to use.

GINGER

To use fresh root ginger, cut off the required amount, skin it and grate on the small blades of a hand grater. Fresh ginger also keeps well in the fridge.

GRAM FLOUR

Gram flour is readily available from Asian shops and larger supermarkets. It is a fine, yellow-coloured flour, made from small dark chickpeas (chana) which are split, husked and ground into a fine powder. Gram flour has a nutty flavour and is used in many recipes.

OIL

Use any brand of sunflower, corn or groundnut oil for all the recipes, except for some of the sweets which require ghee.

PEANUTS

Several recipes in this book include peanuts. As some people suffer from a dangerous allergic reaction to peanuts, you should always warn guests about dishes containing them.

Peanuts can be ground in a coffee grinder or food processor.

TAMARIND SAUCE

Tamarind Sauce (p. 93) can be frozen in ice cube trays. Simply store the frozen cubes in a plastic box in the freezer and defrost before use.

TOMATOES

To skin fresh tomatoes, make a slit on each one with a sharp knife, and soak in hot water for 30–60 seconds. The skins should then slip off easily. If there is no time to skin and chop the tomatoes, the clever solution is to cut each one in half and grate the inside flesh using a hand grater.

COOKING METHODS

PREPARING INGREDIENTS

It's important to wash and chop all your ingredients – ginger, chilli, garlic, onion, coriander and vegetables – before starting each recipe. Arrange all the prepared ingredients, and any spices you will need, on a tray next to the cooking area before you begin.

DEEP-FRYING

This can be done in a deep frying pan, a wok or a karahi. You can tell that the oil is hot enough when a piece of bread browns in 30 seconds.

The traditional Indian cast-iron karahi gives even heat, cooks the food fast, and helps it stay crisp. It is also believed that a little bit of iron, which is good for the body, is stirred in with the food. However I use a non-stick wok which has most of the advantages of the karahi but is easier to clean.

Dry-Roasting

This cooking method is often used when preparing whole spices for spice mixtures such as garam masala (p. 9). Simply heat a non-stick frying pan and stir-fry the whole spices, without any oil, for a few minutes, until the colour changes.

'Kalam kshetram matram swatmyam dravya gurulaghvam svabalam Gnatva yobhyavharyam bhunkte kim bhaishjestasya.'

('Those who eat after considering time, place, quantity, and the food's lightness or heaviness, together with the energy it gives, do not require any medicines.')

From a Jain holy book *Prashamrati*, written in the first century AD by a famous monk called Umaswati.

Courtesy Vinod Kapashi

SPICES

IN INDIAN cooking spices play a very prominent role, imparting flavour, aroma and colour, as well as fulfilling digestive and medicinal purposes. (The art of Ayurveda medicine is practised using all the spices and herbs).

A successful curry combines various spices in the right proportions. The key to making good Indian food is the fact that each spice is freshly ground and individually mixed according to the composition of the dish.

Spices are expensive, so buy them in small amounts in order to keep the aromatic and volatile oils fresh.

It's worth investing in a spice tin if you do not already have one. The usual spices to store in the tin are salt, chilli powder, turmeric, dhana jeera, mustard seeds, cumin seeds and asafoetida (keep the asafoetida in a small bottle as well as the tin so that it does not overpower the other spices).

There are many reference books on spices, their history and medicinal qualities, so here is just a brief outline of some of the principal spices and their daily use:

AJWAIN (AJMA SEEDS)

These have a similar flavour to thyme and are mainly used in Indian savouries, especially recipes using gram flour. In India, the seeds are a household remedy for indigestion.

AMCHOOR

This powder is made from dried unripe Indian mangoes. It gives a sour taste and is available from Asian shops.

ASAFOETIDA

Asafoetida is a dried brownish-yellow resin, sold in lumps or powder form. The powder form is combined with rice powder to prevent it from lumping. It has a strong characteristic aroma, which is due to the sulphur compounds present in the volatile oils. Asafoetida is both a diuretic and a digestive and is mainly used with pulses to prevent flatulence.

CARDAMOM

Cardamom pods and seeds are used in both sweet and savoury dishes. The flavour is pungent and highly aromatic. Indians love to use cardamom as a breath sweetener and the seeds are chewed after a meal to aid digestion.

CHAT MASALA

This has a sharp sour taste and is used in fruit and vegetable salads. Ready-mixed chat masala is available from Asian shops. If you are unable to find it, you can make your own by mixing all the ingredients listed below:

1 teaspoon salt
½ teaspoon freshly ground black
  pepper
½ teaspoon rock salt

1 teaspoon cumin seeds, dry-roasted
  and ground
½ teaspoon asafoetida
1 teaspoon amchoor (mango powder)

Store in an air-tight bottle and use as required.

CHILLIES

Chilli powder is the dynamite that imparts heat and colour to Indian food. The burning sensation caused by fresh chillies is due to a substance called capsaicin which is concentrated in the seeds and the membrane, so if you prefer a milder taste you can remove the seeds and the top quarter of the chilli before use. Chillies contain high levels of vitamins A and C, and also aid digestion.

CINNAMON

This is nature's most aromatic spice and an important ingredient of garam masala (see page 9).

CLOVES

These dark brown, dried, unopened buds contain an essential oil which acts as a mild anaesthetic, is a strong antiseptic and is used for preserving food. Cloves are also an ingredient of garam masala (see opposite).

CORIANDER

The fresh green leaves of coriander are used as a herb. Coriander seeds are used as a spice and are antibacterial. They are also an appetiser and stimulate digestion. When a recipe calls for crushed coriander seeds this can easily be done using a rolling pin or a mortar and pestle.

CUMIN

This spice is indispensable when cooking curries. Cumin is a very old spice, and cumin seeds were found in the Pyramids. Cumin is also an important ingredient of garam masala (see opposite). To make your own **roasted cumin powder**, dry-roast the seeds in a non-stick frying pan without any oil until lightly brown, cool and grind in a coffee grinder, and store in an air-tight bottle.

DHANA JEERA

This is a ready-made mixture of coriander seeds and cumin seeds ground together and sold in Asian shops. If you prefer to prepare your own, mix the equivalent of 2 teaspoons ground coriander to ½ teaspoon ground cumin. Use a lot of this spice to flavour and thicken curries.

FENNEL

Fennel is both a herb and a spice. The seeds are an ingredient of Mukhwas, a chew to aid digestion and sweeten the breath.

FENUGREEK (METHI)

Fenugreek is both a herb and a spice. It is a good digestive aid and is said to be an aphrodisiac. The seeds are used whole or ground for pickles and curry powder. If fresh fenugreek leaves are unavailable, you may be able to find dried ones. These just need to be soaked for 5 minutes and rinsed before use, though they lack the flavour of fresh fenugreek.

GARAM MASALA

The name of this spice mixture means 'warming spices'. Each family selects its own combination of spices, dry-roasts and grinds it. The flavour of home-made garam masala is much better than bought ones. To make your own, you will need:

1 tablespoon cumin seeds	1 tablespoon black peppercorns
1 tablespoon cinnamon sticks, broken into small pieces	2 teaspoons cloves

Dry-roast all the spices in a non-stick frying pan for 4–5 minutes, until the colour changes to dark brown and a spicy aroma is released. When the mixture is cool, after about 10 minutes, grind it in a coffee grinder. Sieve and store in an air-tight bottle.

GINGER

Fresh ginger is used in curries and ground ginger is used as a spice. Fresh ginger is a root with a strong, slightly biting flavour. Scrape or peel the skin before grating or chopping finely. It can be stored in a fridge for a long time in a paper bag. Fresh ginger is used in many Indian recipes.

MUSTARD

Small dark mustard seeds have good digestive properties. Always add mustard seeds when the oil is hot, and wait for the seeds to splutter and release their flavour before adding the other ingredients.

NUTMEG AND MACE

Mace is the orange-coloured lacy covering that surrounds a nutmeg seed. Powdered mace is used sparingly in sweets and some savoury dishes, as it has a very strong flavour.

The nutmeg lies within the shell of the seed. The seeds are cracked open and the nutmeg is removed. Nutmeg should be grated as required, as it soon loses its flavour.

Pav Bhaji Masala

Pav bhaji masala is a mixture of chillies, coriander, cumin, ginger, cloves, black pepper, bay leaves, amchoor, asafoetida and salt. It is easier to buy pav bhaji masala (which is sold in most Asian stores) than to make your own.

Saffron

Saffron is an 'aristocrat' amongst spices and is very expensive. It is the dried stigma and part of the style of the crocus flower. Saffron is used for colouring rice and savoury dishes, and its flavour and bouquet is essential for festive cooking and elaborate Indian sweets.

Turmeric

Ground turmeric is a deep yellow fine powder made from the turmeric root. It is famous for its bright yellow colour and is used in curries to colour the sauce. A small amount is enough to flavour and colour a dish; too much will make the food bitter.

CHAPTER ONE

STARTERS AND
SNACKS

A TRADITIONAL Indian meal does not have three set courses. Instead, all the dishes are served and eaten simultaneously – one picks and chooses a little of each dish as one wishes.

However the trend is now changing, perhaps for the better, as I often feel the starters are the best part of a meal. At parties, 'finger food' starters can be a great conversation piece, inspiring the guests to exchange cooking ideas and recipes. (I have not yet sat at a formal or informal meal when recipes have not been discussed.) Often, just talking about food and visualising it gets the saliva flowing – a perfect appetiser. Also, while the starters are being served, you have time to warm up the main meal.

In this chapter I have tried to select a really colourful and exciting range of recipes. I have included some cold starters, like Chat Masala Salad and Khandvi, and some new dishes, like Paneer Tikka, and Masala-Spiced Sugar Snap Peas and Cashew Nuts.

Many of these dishes also make excellent snacks, or light meals when served with breads, rice and salad.

All the recipes in this chapter are suitable for vegans apart from those on pages 12, 14 and 20.

· PANEER TIKKA ·

This dish has been inspired by my love for paneer, a kind of Indian cheese which resembles cottage cheese.

Ready-prepared paneer is sold in chilled compartments in major super-markets and Asian shops. Once opened, use the paneer within a day or freeze it. If you prefer to make your own, a simple recipe is given on p. 46.

This colourful starter is very quick to prepare, and can also be served as a main course with salad and bread. Yogurt and Onion Chutney (p. 96) goes well with it.

SERVES 4

2 tablespoons oil
1 teaspoon cumin seeds
100g (4oz) mushrooms, wiped and sliced
2 medium-sized potatoes, peeled, boiled and cut into small cubes
175g (6oz) paneer, cut into small cubes
1 teaspoon salt

lots of freshly ground black pepper
1 teaspoon tandoori masala (ready-mixed powder masala rather than paste)
1 tablespoon chopped coriander leaves
lemon juice
1 teaspoon mint, chopped fresh or bottled (optional)

1. Heat the oil in a wok or a deep frying pan. When hot, add the cumin seeds and sliced mushrooms, and sauté for 4–6 minutes.

2. Add the potatoes, paneer, salt, black pepper, tandoori masala, coriander, lemon juice to taste, and mint if using. Cook for 6–8 minutes, stirring occasionally.

3. Serve hot or cold on individual plates.

· ONION BHAJIS ·

The famous onion bhajis are easy to prepare. Serve them with Tamarind Sauce (p. 93) or Red Pepper Chutney (p. 94).

MAKES 8 BHAJIS

½ big onion, weighing approximately 350g (12oz), (Spanish is best), cut in half again, peeled and sliced
5 tablespoons gram flour
1 tablespoon oil
1½ teaspoons salt
1 teaspoon sugar

1 teaspoon lemon juice
1 teaspoon ground cumin
1 teaspoon chopped green chilli
1 tablespoon chopped fresh coriander
¼ teaspoon baking powder
2–3 tablespoons water
extra oil for deep-frying

1. Mix all the above ingredients together in a bowl, except the extra oil, and let the mixture rest for 15 minutes. The onion will weep and make enough liquid to bind the mixture well. If it is still too thick, add 1 tablespoon extra water but do not make it too runny.

2. Mix and stir well by hand.

3. Heat the extra oil in a wok or a deep frying pan until a piece of bread browns in 30 seconds.

4. Use a dessertspoon to drop small spoonfuls of the mixture gently into the hot oil and deep-fry the fritters till they are golden all over.

· KHANDVI ·

These delicate gram flour rolls, spiced with flavoured oil, coconut and coriander, make a really stunning cold starter. This recipe brings back memories of my childhood, for my mother was expert at making them. It is an acquired art, so if you do not succeed the first time, please try again. Once you have learnt the technique, this will become one of the most impressive dishes in your repertoire.

SERVES 4

4 tablespoons gram flour
1 tablespoon natural yogurt
1 heaped teaspoon salt
¼ teaspoon ground turmeric
1 teaspoon chilli powder
2 tablespoons oil
6–8 curry leaves

1 teaspoon mustard seeds
2 teaspoons sesame seeds
¼ teaspoon asafoetida
1 tablespoon desiccated or fresh grated
  coconut
1 tablespoon coriander leaves

1. Use an electric mixer or a whisk to mix the gram flour, yogurt and 500ml (17fl oz) water. Strain the mixed liquid and add the salt, turmeric and ½ teaspoon red chilli powder.

2. In a heavy-based saucepan, heat this liquid over a medium heat for 5 minutes. Stir a few times.

3. As soon as it bubbles, lower the heat a little and start stirring with a wooden spoon. Stir for 15–20 minutes, until thick. Make sure it stays smooth – you will have to keep stirring to prevent it from lumping. Remove from the heat.

4. Put 2 tablespoons of the mixture on a tray or a flat surface and spread the paste thinly, using the back of a wide spoon – the thinner you spread it the better. Repeat until all the paste is spread, using several trays if necessary.

5. When cold (in 3–5 minutes), cut into strips 2.5cm (1 inch) wide and roll up into mini Swiss rolls. Arrange on a serving tray. Sprinkle the remaining ½ teaspoon red chilli powder on them.

6. Now heat the oil in a small saucepan. When hot, add the curry leaves, mustard seeds, sesame seeds and asafoetida. Pour this flavoured oil over the rolls, decorate with the grated or desiccated coconut and the coriander leaves, and serve cold.

· CUMIN CASSAVA ·

Cassava is a root vegetable and, like potato, is part of the staple diet of Africans in East and West Africa. Fresh cassava, barbecued on an open fire, smothered in salt, chilli powder and lime juice, is a taste not to be forgotten. In Britain it is widely available, fresh or frozen, from Asian shops.

This simple stir-fry recipe brings out the earthy flavour of cassava. Serve it as a starter or part of a light meal.

SERVES 4

450g (1lb) cassava (fresh or frozen)
1–2 tablespoons oil
2 teaspoons cumin seeds
1 long green chilli, sliced

salt
lemon juice
1 lemon, sliced

1. If using fresh cassava, peel off the hard outer skin, wash and cut into 5cm (2 inch) pieces. Boil for 6–8 minutes and drain. If using frozen cassava, boil for 4–6 minutes (it comes in ready-prepared bite-size pieces).

2. In a wok or a deep frying pan, heat the oil and add the cumin seeds, cassava pieces and chilli. Add salt and lemon juice to taste, and stir for 6 minutes until lightly browned.

3. Serve hot, garnished with slices of lemon.

· SPICY SWEETCORN ·

This spicy, tangy sweetcorn mixture makes a tasty and unusual starter.

SERVES 2

6 tablespoons tinned or frozen
  sweetcorn kernels
1 tablespoon oil
1 teaspoon mustard seeds
1 small green chilli, de-seeded and
  chopped
1 teaspoon salt

1 teaspoon chilli powder
1 teaspoon lemon juice
1 tablespoon chopped fresh coriander
1 small onion, peeled and finely
  chopped
a few potato crisps, crushed

1. If using frozen sweetcorn, boil for 4 minutes and drain well.

2. In a pan, heat the oil, and add the mustard seeds. When the seeds splutter, add the sweetcorn.

3. Cook for 2 minutes, then add the green chilli and the salt, chilli powder, lemon juice and chopped coriander. Cook for a further 5–7 minutes.

4. Serve the sweetcorn mixture on individual plates, topped with some finely chopped onion and a few crushed potato crisps.

· COLD CORIANDER TRIANGLES ·

This novel way of using fresh green coriander is popular with young and old alike, makes an excellent snack and can also be served as party 'finger food'.

1. Prepare 1 quantity Coriander Chutney (p. 92).

2. Using thin sliced white or brown bread, spread one slice with very little butter or margarine and another slice with coriander chutney. Make a sandwich, trim off the crusts and slice into 4 triangles. Repeat until you have your desired quantity.

3. Serve cold with lettuce leaves and crisps.

· QUICK SAMOSAS ·

Samosas are one of the best-known Indian snacks, but they are time-consuming to make. My variation uses a similar filling, between two slices of toasted bread. Add more garam masala if you like your samosas hot, and serve them with Spicy Tomato Chutney (p. 94).

SERVES 4

2 large potatoes, peeled
oil
1 large carrot, peeled
1 onion, peeled
1 teaspoon cumin seeds
1 teaspoon grated fresh ginger
1 teaspoon chopped green chilli
2 tablespoons fresh or frozen peas

1 teaspoon salt
1 teaspoon garam masala (p. 9)
a little sugar (optional)
lemon juice to taste
1 tablespoon chopped fresh coriander
about 8 thin slices of bread
butter or margarine

---

1. Cut the potatoes into very small cubes and deep-fry in a wok or karahi until golden (or use boiled potato cut into cubes).

2. Cut the carrot into very small cubes and chop the onion.

3. Heat 1 tablespoon oil in a deep pan. When hot, add the cumin seeds and sauté the chopped onion for 3–4 minutes.

4. Add the ginger, chilli, carrots, peas, salt, garam masala, sugar if using, and lemon juice. Cover the pan and sauté for 10 minutes. Add the potato and coriander. Mix well and season to taste.

5. Butter one slice of bread, place it butter-side down in a sandwich toaster, spread with 1–2 tablespoons filling, and cover it with another slice of bread butter-side up. Toast until golden on both sides, cut in half diagonally, and serve hot. Repeat with remaining bread and filling.

—— VARIATION ——

Another quick way of making samosas is using ready-made puff pastry.

✦ Prepare a similar vegetable stuffing as above, using any combination of vegetables.

✦ Roll out a small thin piece of puff pastry, place a spoonful of vegetable stuffing on one half, and fold over and seal the edges using a fork. Make a couple of slits on top for the warm vapour to escape.

✦ Bake for 20 minutes at 200°C/400°F (Gas Mark 6).

✦ Serve hot or cold with Spicy Tomato Chutney (p. 94) or Coriander Chutney (p. 92).

Hot Toasted Cheese and · Coriander Sandwich ·

You can make this appetising dish using a sandwich toaster or an ordinary grill.

--- SERVES 2 ---

3 tablespoons grated cheese (Cheddar or a mixture of Cheddar, Gruyère and Emmenthal)

3 teaspoons Coriander Chutney (p. 92)

salt and freshly ground black pepper to taste

2–3 spring onions, finely sliced

1 small tomato, chopped

1 teaspoon roasted cumin powder (p. 8, optional)

4 slices of bread

butter or margarine (optional)

fresh green chillies

a few sprigs of fresh coriander

potato crisps

1. Mix the cheese, chutney, seasoning, spring onions, tomato, and cumin powder if using.

2. Spread half the mixture on one slice of bread and cover with another slice. Repeat with the other half of the mixture and toast the sandwiches on both sides under the grill. If using a sandwich toaster, you will need to butter the first slice of bread, place it butter-side down in the toaster, spread over the filling, and cover it with another slice of bread butter-side up.

3. Before serving, slit open the sandwiches in the middle, and the melted cheese will ooze out. Serve hot, garnished with some long green chillies, a few sprigs of coriander and some potato crisps.

· GRAM FLOUR PANCAKES ·

These Gujarati pancakes, made from gram (chickpea) flour and known as pudlas, are a popular, light, savoury lunch dish. Serve them with Cucumber Raita (p. 102).

MAKES 6 PANCAKES

225g (8oz) gram flour
1 teaspoon chilli powder
1 teaspoon cumin seeds, dry-roasted
1 teaspoon ajwain seeds
1 teaspoon salt

¼ teaspoon ground turmeric
4 spring onions, chopped
1 tomato, peeled, de-seeded and diced
2 tablespoons chopped fresh coriander
oil

1. Sift the gram flour into a large bowl, stir in the remaining ingredients, including 1 tablespoon oil, and then beat in about 250ml (9fl oz) cold water to form a thick pouring batter. Leave to settle for about 15 minutes.

2. Brush an 18cm (7 inch) heavy-based non-stick frying pan or omelette pan with a little oil.

3. Pour in a large spoonful of the batter, tilting it to coat the whole pan, and cook for about 2 minutes. Carefully turn over, add ½ teaspoon oil and cook for about another 2 minutes. Repeat the process to make 5 more pancakes.

4. These pancakes can be made earlier and reheated in a hot oven, wrapped in foil, just before serving.

—— VARIATION ——

For **Chutney Pudlas**, prepare the batter as above but omit the spring onion and tomato.

✦ Cook the pancakes as described.

✦ Before serving, spread 2 teaspoons Mint Chutney (p. 92) over each pancake and roll it up like a Swiss roll. Serve the rolled-up pancakes whole, or cut into 5cm (2 inch rolls), and speared on cocktail sticks for party 'finger food'. This is my favourite way of eating these pancakes.

· VEGETABLE BURGERS ·

In Bombay and Delhi, in the evenings, as soon as business comes to an end, the street vendors take over. In the light from their portable lanterns, these vegetable burgers (known as pav bhaji) and other mouth-watering dishes are cooked on huge griddles. The whole scene, of people dressed in brightly coloured clothes, walking with their hot food through the main streets, has an almost carnival air. Most people have a light supper at their homes and then go to eat pav bhaji at their favourite vendor's stall. It is a treat not to be missed. On my various visits to Bombay, my uncle made a point of taking us to sample their wares and the memory still lingers.

Pav means bread and bhaji is a curry. A variety of vegetables are steamed and kept in separate trays so that each customer can choose their favourite combination, adding spices to their personal taste. This is an ideal meal on its own, a great dish for parties and a perfect dish to cook for a barbecue. Ready-made pav bhaji masala is sold in boxes in most Asian shops.

SERVES 6

2 big potatoes, peeled
1 large carrot
2–4 florets cauliflower
2 tablespoons fresh or frozen peas
2–4 tablespoons butter or margarine
1 onion, peeled and chopped
4 fresh tomatoes, skinned (p. 4) and chopped
2–4 garlic cloves, peeled and chopped (optional)

1–2 green chillies, chopped
1–2 teaspoons pav bhaji masala (p. 10) to taste
1 teaspoon salt (or to taste)
1 tablespoon finely chopped fresh coriander
1 teaspoon lemon juice
6 soft burger buns

1. Chop the potatoes, carrot and cauliflower into small pieces and steam, together with the peas, for 12–15 minutes, until soft.

2. In a wok or a deep frying pan, melt 2 tablespoons butter and sauté the onion till soft. Add the tomatoes, garlic and chillies, and cook for 4 minutes. Add pav bhaji masala and salt to taste, and stir well. Add the vegetables, mash the mixture as you keep stirring, and cook very fast for just a few minutes. Add the chopped coriander and season to taste with lemon juice.

3. Cut the buns in half, spread thinly with butter or margarine and brown on a griddle or under a grill. Spoon the spicy vegetable mixture into each bun and serve hot.

· SPINACH OR FENUGREEK FRITTERS ·

This is a quick dish using very basic ingredients – fenugreek (small-leafed Indian spinach), gram flour, semolina and spices. Use small spinach leaves if fresh fenugreek is unavailable, but increase the quantities of spices and lemon juice.

Serve these fritters with Cucumber Raita (p. 102) or Spicy Tomato Chutney (p. 94) or as a savoury dish with the main meal.

MAKES 12–16 FRITTERS

6 tablespoons gram flour

2 tablespoons semolina

2 tablespoons chopped fresh fenugreek leaves

1 tablespoon chopped fresh coriander

2.5cm (1 inch) piece banana, chopped

1 green chilli, de-seeded and chopped

1 teaspoon cumin seeds, dry-roasted

½ teaspoon ajwain seeds (optional)

¼ teaspoon baking powder

1 teaspoon salt

2 teaspoons lemon juice

oil

1. Combine all the ingredients, except the oil, with 2–3 tablespoons water. Beat by hand or use a food processor to form a thick batter and set aside for 20 minutes.

2. Heat some oil in a wok or karahi until a cube of bread browns in 30 seconds.

3. Drop the mixture gently in small spoonfuls and fry for 2–4 minutes, turning occasionally. Complete the frying in 2–3 batches, depending on the size of the pan.

4. Drain the fritters on kitchen paper and serve hot.

· COCONUT SOUP ·

This simple dish makes a fragrant and exotic first course. Or you could serve it with bread or a rice dish as a light lunch.

SERVES 4

400ml (14fl oz) tinned coconut milk
2 teaspoons cornflour
1 small potato, peeled
3–4 radishes, washed
1 small carrot, peeled
1 tablespoon oil
2 cinnamon sticks
1 teaspoon grated fresh ginger
1 tablespoon frozen peas

1 whole green chilli
2 tablespoons desiccated or fresh grated
  coconut
1 teaspoon salt (or to taste)
1 teaspoon sugar
½ teaspoon garam masala (p. 9)
1 tablespoon chopped fresh coriander
chilli powder

1. In a jug mix the coconut milk and cornflour with 600ml (1 pint) water. Cut the potato into small cubes, and thinly slice the radishes and carrot.

2. Heat the oil in a pan, and add the cinnamon sticks, ginger, potato, carrot, radish and peas. Stir-fry for 3 minutes.

3. Add the coconut milk mixture and bring to the boil. Stir well, add the whole green chilli, the desiccated or fresh grated coconut, the salt, sugar and garam masala. Simmer, uncovered, for 10–15 minutes.

4. Ladle into 4 bowls and garnish with finely chopped coriander and a sprinkling of chilli powder.

Masala-Spiced Sugar Snap
· Peas & Cashew Nuts ·

The subtle sweetness of sugar snap peas and cashew nuts blends very well with the spices in this recipe. Serve it as a fresh, crunchy starter or even a lunch dish with Cumin Potatoes (p. 28) or Sesame Potatoes (p. 29) and a salad. You could use mangetout instead of sugar snap peas.

——— SERVES 2 ———

1 tablespoon oil
½ teaspoon cumin seeds
100g (4oz) sugar snap peas
50g (2oz) cashew nuts
1 tablespoon Coriander Chutney (p. 92)
  or 1 tablespoon chopped fresh
  coriander and 1 green chilli, chopped

½ teaspoon salt
½ teaspoon chilli powder
lemon juice

1. Heat the oil in a wok or a deep frying pan. When hot, add the cumin seeds, peas and cashew nuts.

2. Stir for 6 minutes, add the coriander chutney (or the fresh coriander and chilli), the salt and chilli powder, and cook for a further 3 minutes.

3. Season to taste with lemon juice and serve hot or cold.

· CHAT MASALA SALAD ·

Chat is the name given in India to any fruit or vegetable salad spiced with chat masala. The hot spices coupled with fresh fruit and vegetables make a very refreshing starter. Use any fruits you like which are readily available. Grapes, kiwi fruit, mandarins, guavas, pears and stoned cherries make a very interesting chat.

SERVES 2

1 green dessert apple
2 new potatoes, scrubbed and boiled
10cm (4 inch) piece cucumber
lemon juice

1 small raw green mango, skinned and
  shredded (optional)
2 teaspoons chat masala (p. 7)
lettuce leaves

1. Chop the apple, potatoes and cucumber into equal bite-size cubes and sprinkle with lemon juice. Mix well, and add the shredded mango if using.

2. Add the ready-made chat masala and mix.

3. Cover well and refrigerate for approximately ½ hour to allow all the spices to marinate together.

4. Serve on a bed of lettuce leaves.

CLOCKWISE FROM THE TOP: Aubergine and Green Lentil Pullav (page 74), Avocado and Tomato Raita (page 103), Cornmeal Puris (page 85)

CHAPTER TWO

POTATO DISHES

IN THE COURSE of writing this book, I decided that potato dishes deserved a chapter of their own. There are so many ways of cooking potatoes and most households usually have some in the cupboard, so this vegetable is a good starting point for anyone learning to cook with spices.

Potato curries can be served as part of a main meal, to be eaten with naan or rice. However, most of these dishes can also make a light lunch or starter, if served with chutneys.

The recipes range from simple stir-fries (such as Cumin Potatoes and Sesame Potatoes) to more elaborate concoctions, like Potatoes in Spicy Coconut Milk. Some of the dishes are well known and cooked by most Indian families, while others (such as Steamed Coriander Potatoes) have been conceived while I have been working on this book.

There is only one recipe in this chapter that is not suitable for a vegan diet – Potatoes in Spiced Yogurt on page 33.

CLOCKWISE FROM THE TOP: Chat Masala Salad (page 26), Spicy Potato Balls (page 32), Khandvi (page 14), Coriander Chutney (page 92)

· CUMIN POTATOES ·

This simple starter really whets the appetite.

——— SERVES 2 AS A LIGHT MEAL; 4 AS A STARTER ———

450g (1lb) potatoes, peeled
2 tablespoons oil or melted butter
1 tablespoon cumin seeds
1 tablespoon fresh ginger, peeled and
   cut into small matchsticks

1 long green chilli, thinly sliced
1 teaspoon salt
a little freshly ground black pepper
1 teaspoon lemon or lime juice
a few fresh coriander leaves

1. Boil the potatoes, drain, peel and cut into thick chips.

2. In a wok or a deep frying pan, heat the oil or butter, and add the cumin and ginger. Sizzle and stir for 2–3 minutes, then add the potatoes, chilli, salt, pepper and lemon or lime juice. Sauté for at least 5 minutes more until all the potato pieces are covered with the spicy mixture.

3. Garnish with the fresh coriander and serve hot or cold.

· SESAME POTATOES ·

The combination of just a few spices, stir-fried with the potato, gives it an exciting new taste, and the sesame seeds add a wonderful crunchy texture. Serve this dish cold, with watercress or mixed salad leaves and plain yogurt or Yogurt and Onion Chutney (p. 96) as a dip.

SERVES 2 AS A LIGHT MEAL; 4 AS A STARTER

450g (1lb) potatoes, peeled
2 tablespoons oil
1 teaspoon cumin seeds
2 tablespoons sesame seeds

1 teaspoon coriander seeds, crushed
1 teaspoon salt (or more to taste)
2 teaspoons freshly ground black
    pepper

1. Boil the potatoes, drain, peel and cut into cubes. If using new potatoes, do not peel and keep them whole.

2. In a wok or a deep frying pan, heat 2 tablespoons oil, then add the cumin, sesame seeds, crushed coriander seeds and the potato. Stir-fry for 3–5 minutes, mixing well.

3. Season with salt and plenty of freshly ground pepper, and leave to get cold before serving.

· STIR-FRIED POTATO & CORIANDER ·

The combination of dry coriander seeds and fresh coriander leaves gives this potato dish an instant oriental flavour. Serve as a light meal, with bread and salad, or as part of a main meal.

SERVES 2

2 large potatoes, peeled
1 tablespoon oil
1 teaspoon coriander seeds, crushed
1 tablespoon peanut kernels (optional)

1 tablespoon fresh coriander leaves
1 teaspoon salt (or less to taste)
½ teaspoon chilli powder
1 teaspoon lemon juice

1. Boil the potatoes, drain and cut into small cubes.

2. In a wok or a deep frying pan, heat the oil over a medium heat. Stir in the coriander seeds, and peanuts if using, and cook till brown, for about 5 minutes. Add the potatoes, fresh coriander leaves, salt and chilli powder and sauté for 5–8 minutes.

3. Season with lemon juice and serve hot or cold.

· POTATO FRITTERS ·

These delicious, quick fritters are ideal 'finger food' for a party. Serve hot or cold with Coriander Chutney (p. 92) and Tamarind Sauce (p. 93).

MAKES 25–30 FRITTERS

1 × 225g (8oz) potato, peeled
3 tablespoons gram flour
1 green chilli, de-seeded and chopped
1 tablespoon chopped fresh coriander
1 teaspoon salt.
1 teaspoon chilli powder

1 teaspoon roasted cumin powder (p. 8)
½ teaspoon ajwain seeds
2 teaspoons lemon juice
oil

1. Slice the potato into thin rounds, using a mandolin if you have one.

2. Whisk all the remaining ingredients together, with 1 tablespoon oil and 4 tablespoons cold water, to form a smooth runny batter, rather like pancake batter. Mix very well.

3. Heat some oil in a wok or deep frying pan until a cube of bread browns in 30 seconds. Dip each potato slice into the batter and deep-fry until golden on both sides (about 2–4 minutes). Drain on kitchen paper.

· SPICY POTATO BALLS ·

This recipe may look long and complicated but potato balls are the easiest and tastiest fritters to cook. For extra taste and visual appeal, make a small slit in each potato ball and spoon over a little Coriander Chutney (p. 92) and Tamarind Sauce (p. 93).

SERVES 4

2–3 potatoes, peeled and boiled
2 teaspoons salt
½ teaspoon roasted cumin powder (p. 8)
½ teaspoon sugar
½ teaspoon garam masala (p. 9)
1 small green chilli, de-seeded and chopped

2 tablespoons chopped fresh coriander
1 teaspoon lemon juice
1 tablespoon cashew nuts, broken into pieces
1 tablespoon sultanas (optional)
3 tablespoons gram flour
1 teaspoon chilli powder
oil

---

1. Mash the boiled potatoes, then add 1 teaspoon salt, cumin, sugar, garam masala, chilli, 1 tablespoon chopped fresh coriander, lemon juice, cashew nuts, and sultanas if using. Mix well so that the spices are spread evenly, then roll the mixture into 2.5cm (1 inch) balls.

2. In a bowl, mix together the gram flour, 1 teaspoon salt, chilli powder, 1 tablespoon chopped fresh coriander, 1 tablespoon oil and a little cold water to form a thick pancake batter.

3. Heat some oil in a wok or deep frying pan until a cube of bread browns in 30 seconds. Dip each potato ball in the gram flour batter and deep-fry till golden. Serve hot or cold.

VARIATION

A new trend, making a great starter for a strong stomach, is to use the above potato mixture to make **stuffed mild green poblano chillies**.

✦ Make the potato mixture and gram flour batter as above.

✦ Then slit each chilli on one side, lengthways, remove the seeds, and stuff with the potato mixture. Dip it in the gram flour batter and deep-fry till golden.

· POTATOES IN SPICED YOGURT ·

This is a simple recipe (assembled just before serving to retain its crispness), but the addition of spiced yogurt, Coriander Chutney and Tamarind Sauce turns it into a very tasty, mouth-watering and decorative dish. Sev are the cooked thin gram flour noodles which are an important ingredient of Bombay mix. They are available, ready-made in packets, from Asian shops.

SERVES 2

2 × 100g (4oz) potatoes, peeled and boiled
oil
4 tablespoons natural yogurt
1 teaspoon salt
½ teaspoon roasted cumin powder (p. 8)

½ teaspoon chat masala (p. 7)
1 tablespoon Tamarind Sauce (p. 93)
2 teaspoons Coriander Chutney (p. 92)
½ teaspoon chilli powder
a handful of fresh coriander leaves
a handful of ready-made gram flour sev (optional)

1. Slice the boiled potatoes into 1cm (½ inch) thick slices and heat some oil in a wok or deep frying pan. Either deep-fry the potato slices like chips or sauté until golden.

2. Assemble all the other ingredients separately.

3. Just before serving, arrange the cooked potato slices on a big serving dish. Spice the yogurt to your taste with the salt, roasted cumin powder and chat masala, and spread it generously over the potato slices. Now spread the tamarind sauce and coriander chutney onto all the potatoes. Finally, sprinkle over the chilli powder and fresh coriander leaves, and garnish with sev if using.

· RED GARLIC POTATOES ·

This is a popular snack or starter. It may look hot but it is very mild.

SERVES 4

450g (1lb) potatoes
4–6 garlic cloves, peeled
450g (1lb) fresh tomatoes
2 tablespoons oil
1 teaspoon cumin seeds

salt
2 teaspoons tomato purée (optional)
a large handful of potato crisps, crushed
1 tablespoon fresh grated coconut
 (optional)

1. Peel the potatoes and cut them into big chunks. Chop or crush the garlic. Then chop the fresh tomatoes, blend them in a liquidiser or food processor, and sieve the liquid.

2. Heat the oil in a big pan. When it is hot, add the cumin seeds and garlic and cook for 2 minutes. Add the sieved blended tomatoes and bring to the boil.

3. Add the potatoes, salt to taste, and enough water to cook the potatoes. If required, add the tomato purée (to give added colour to the dish). Cook covered, until the potatoes are very soft and the red gravy has thickened.

4. Add a big handful of crushed potato crisps, and the fresh grated coconut if you wish, and serve immediately.

· STEAMED CORIANDER POTATOES ·

While writing this book, I was inspired to try this recipe. It's so easy yet so original and decorative; I hope it becomes one of your favourites too. Serve it warm or cold as a starter on individual plates, with some baby spinach leaves or lamb's lettuce.

—————————————————— SERVES 2 ——————————————————

1 × 225g (8oz) potato, peeled
2 tablespoons Coriander Chutney (p. 92)
2 tablespoons fresh grated coconut
½ teaspoon salt (or more to taste)
½ teaspoon chilli powder

1–2 tablespoons oil
6–8 curry leaves
½ teaspoon mustard seeds
½ teaspoon cumin seeds
1 tablespoon sesame seeds

•

1. Cut the potato into 5mm (¼ inch) thick rounds. Prepare the Coriander Chutney as on p. 92. (If you have ice cubes of Coriander Chutney, defrost 2 cubes.)

2. Mix 1½ tablespoons grated coconut with the coriander chutney, sandwich between 2 equal-sized potato pieces and arrange on a flat tray, or in a shallow cake tin, ready for steaming. Sprinkle a little salt and chilli powder over the potato slices. Then use a steamer to steam the tray for 15–20 minutes. If you do not have a steamer, balance the tray over a large pan of boiling water, cover the pan with the lid and steam for 15–20 minutes. Carefully transfer the cooked potato slices to a serving dish.

3. Finally, heat the oil in a small pan. When it is hot, add the curry leaves, mustard, cumin and sesame seeds. When the seeds splutter, pour this flavoured oil over the potato slices.

4. Decorate with the remaining grated coconut and serve.

· POTATO AND SHALLOT CURRY ·

This is the most common Indian potato curry. It is excellent served hot with Puris (p. 82) or Stuffed Parathas (p. 88) or rice. If shallots are not available, use baby onions or cut a large onion into big chunks.

SERVES 2

2 big potatoes
4–6 shallots
2 tablespoons oil
2–3 fresh tomatoes, skinned (p. 4) and chopped or 3 tablespoons tinned tomatoes
1 teaspoon cumin seeds

1 teaspoon salt
1 teaspoon chilli powder
¼ teaspoon ground turmeric
1 tablespoon dhana jeera (p. 8)
½ teaspoon sugar
½ teaspoon lemon juice
a few fresh whole coriander leaves

1. Boil the potatoes, drain, peel and cut into big chunks. Soak the shallots in warm water for 5 minutes, and the skin should just peel off.

2. Heat the oil in a pan. When it's hot, add the cumin seeds, tomatoes and shallots; stir for 2–3 minutes. Add the salt, chilli powder, turmeric, dhana jeera, sugar and lemon juice. Mix well.

3. Add the potatoes and 125ml (4fl oz) water, and cook covered for 10–15 minutes until the sauce has thickened.

4. Garnish with a few coriander leaves and serve immediately.

· POTATOES IN SPICY COCONUT MILK ·

This sweet and sour potato curry is a favourite party dish. Have it as part of a main meal, or thin it down with extra water and serve as a soup.

SERVES 4

450g (1lb) potatoes
2–3 tablespoons oil
1 teaspoon mustard seeds
¼ teaspoon asafoetida
6–8 curry leaves
1 teaspoon grated fresh ginger
1 green chilli, chopped
1 teaspoon salt or more

1 teaspoon chilli powder
½ teaspoon sugar
6 tablespoons tinned coconut milk or
    4 tablespoons creamed coconut
1 tablespoon Tamarind Sauce (p. 93)
2 tablespoons peanuts, ground in a
    coffee grinder
2 tablespoons chopped fresh coriander

1. Boil the potatoes, drain, peel and cut into cubes.

2. Heat the oil in a wok or a deep frying pan. When it's hot, add the mustard seeds, asafoetida, curry leaves, ginger and fresh chilli. Stir for 1 minute. Add the potatoes and sauté for 2–3 minutes.

3. Mix in the salt, chilli powder, sugar, coconut milk or creamed coconut and 225ml (8fl oz) water. Bring to the boil, add the tamarind sauce and peanuts, and simmer until the potatoes are well coated in this spicy coconut milk (about 10–12 minutes).

4. Garnish with the chopped fresh coriander and serve.

· POTATO & GREEN PEPPER CURRY ·

Nothing could be easier than this delicious dry curry with all the spices clinging to the vegetables. Serve it as part of a main meal.

SERVES 3–4

1 green pepper
2 big potatoes, boiled and peeled
1 teaspoon salt
1 teaspoon chilli powder
1 tablespoon dhana jeera (p. 8)

½ teaspoon garam masala (p. 9)
¼ teaspoon ground turmeric
2 tablespoons oil
1 teaspoon lemon juice

1. Wash the green pepper and cut it in half. Remove the pith and the seeds and cut into big chunks. Cut the boiled potatoes into the same-sized chunks as the green pepper.

2. In a bowl mix the potatoes, green pepper, salt and spices.

3. Heat the oil in a big pan and add the potato mixture and 225 ml (8 fl oz) water. Stir and cook, covered, over a medium heat. While it is cooking, mash a few pieces of potato to thicken the sauce. In 12–15 minutes, the curry will be ready. Add the lemon juice just before serving.

· POTATO & CAULIFLOWER CURRY ·

Another popular, dry curry, best served as part of a main meal. It combines well with Naan (p. 86) or Bhatura (p. 87) or Puris (p. 82) and Mixed Dal with Fresh Spinach (p. 65), Creamy Mushroom Curry (p. 57) and Cucumber Raita (p. 102).

SERVES 4

450g (1lb) potatoes
1 small cauliflower
2–3 tablespoons oil
1 teaspoon cumin seeds
1 small Spanish onion, peeled and
  chopped
1 long green chilli, de-seeded and
  chopped
2 big tomatoes, skinned (p. 4) and
  chopped or 3 tablespoons tinned
  tomatoes

1 teaspoon salt
1 teaspoon chilli powder
1 teaspoon garam masala (p. 9)
1 tablespoon dhana jeera (p. 8)
¼ teaspoon ground turmeric
1 teaspoon sugar
1 teaspoon lemon juice
1–2 tablespoons natural yogurt
  (optional)
3–4 spring onions, finely sliced

1. Boil the potatoes, peel and cut each one into 4 chunky pieces (if using new potatoes do not peel and keep them whole). Cut the cauliflower into big florets, wash and parboil.

2. Heat the oil in a big pan. When it's hot, add the cumin seeds and the chopped onion. Stir for 4–5 minutes until the onion is soft. Add the chopped fresh chilli, the tomatoes, salt, chilli powder, garam masala, dhana jeera, turmeric, sugar, lemon juice and 3 tablespoons water, and let it cook for 3 minutes.

3. Mix in the potatoes and cauliflower and simmer, covered, for about another 10 minutes.

4. For a thicker sauce, add the yogurt. Garnish with the sliced spring onions and serve.

· SPICY POTATOES & CHICKPEAS ·

This very filling dish is almost a meal on its own, though it can also be served as a quick and popular party dish or snack.

SERVES 4–6

450g (1lb) potatoes, peeled
1 green mango (if available) or
  2 teaspoons lemon juice
225g (8oz) fresh tomatoes, chopped, or
  4 tablespoons tinned tomatoes
1 tablespoon gram flour
1 × 400g (14oz) tin chickpeas
1 Spanish onion, peeled and sliced
3–4 tablespoons oil
1 teaspoon cumin seeds

1 tablespoon tomato purée
1½ teaspoons salt (or to taste)
1 teaspoon chilli powder
1 teaspoon garam masala (p. 9)
2–3 green chillies, de-seeded and cut
  lengthways
1 tablespoon Tamarind Sauce (p. 93)
2 tablespoons desiccated coconut
a few fresh coriander leaves

1. Boil the potatoes, drain and cut into bite-size pieces. If using the green mango, skin and slice it finely. Blend the fresh tomatoes in a liquidiser or food processor, and sieve the liquid.

2. In a bowl mix the gram flour with 3 tablespoons water to form a smooth paste. Open the tin of chickpeas, pour them into a sieve or colander and rinse off the thick liquid.

3. Fry the sliced onion in a big pan in 1 tablespoon oil. Sauté until golden, remove, drain on kitchen paper and set aside to use as a garnish.

4. Add a further 3 tablespoons oil to the pan. When it's hot, add the cumin seeds, half the mango slices if using, the sieved tomatoes and the tomato purée. Bring to the boil and add the salt, chilli powder and garam masala.

5. Cook for 3–4 minutes. Add the gram flour paste and mix well. Add the potatoes and chickpeas and 4 tablespoons water. Cover and cook for a further 10–15 minutes.

6. Add the green chillies, the remaining mango slices if using, the tamarind sauce, coconut and fresh coriander. Garnish with the golden onion slices.

CHAPTER THREE

VEGETABLE DISHES

Supermarkets and Asian grocers nowadays stock an ever-increasing variety of exotic vegetables. In this chapter I want to show how simple it is to prepare flavoursome curries using some of these unusual ingredients.

All the recipes are straightforward, and most have been tried by my students with very successful results. The okra and aubergine dishes are especially quick and will go with any Eastern or Western meal.

The exotic dishes using karela, cluster beans (guvar), drumsticks and fenugreek will excite your palate and become a talking point for your family and friends.

Mushrooms are a very under-rated vegetable and I am glad that they are now being more widely used in Indian cuisine. Why not try cooking Creamy Mushroom Curry to begin with, to get used to the method and the spices? This is a firm favourite with children as well as adults.

The method for preparing paneer looks long but it is really very easy. Paneer is a good source of calcium for vegetarians, and is particularly delicious when cooked with peas in a spicy, creamy sauce, to make the well-known Mogul dish Mattar Paneer.

All the recipes in this chapter can be enjoyed by vegans, apart from those on pages 46, 53 and 57.

· STIR-FRIED OKRA ·

The Indian name for okra is bhindi. It is rich in minerals like magnesium, potassium and sodium and vitamins A and C.

Indians love okra; it is stir-fried, stuffed and cooked in lavish curries. This stir-fry version is my family's favourite way of serving okra and it takes a very short time to prepare. To sweeten the curry, we use jaggery (boiled cane sugar, sold in lumps in oriental shops); brown sugar can be substituted. Buy fresh green okra, avoiding prickly ones with dark blemishes.

SERVES 3–4

450g (1lb) okra
3 tablespoons oil
½ teaspoon mustard seeds
1 teaspoon cumin seeds
1 teaspoon salt (or to taste)
1 teaspoon chilli powder

1 tablespoon dhana jeera (p. 8)
a pinch of ground turmeric
1 dessertspoon jaggery or brown sugar
1 small tomato, finely chopped
a few drops of fresh lemon or lime juice
a few fresh coriander leaves

1. Wash the okra thoroughly, and top and tail. Wipe each okra with kitchen paper and cut into 1cm (½ inch) pieces.

2. Heat the oil in a wok or a deep frying pan. When it's hot, add the mustard and cumin seeds. When the seeds splutter, add the chopped okra and stir gently, taking care not to crush or mash the okra pieces. Stir-fry for 10–15 minutes, until all the stickiness has gone.

3. Season with salt, add the chilli powder, dhana jeera, turmeric, jaggery and chopped tomato, and cook for a further 3–5 minutes.

4. Stir well, add a few drops of lemon or lime juice and serve hot or cold garnished with a few coriander leaves.

Spiced Yoghurt Soup with Fenugreek Dumplings (page 79)

· STUFFED OKRA ·

Another way of serving small, delicate okra is to stuff them with a spicy masala. Serve this dry, spicy dish with a mild Chana Dal (p. 61) or Black-Eye Bean Curry (p. 64) and Potato and Shallot Curry (p. 36) to form part of a main meal.

SERVES 4

450g (1lb) okra
3 tablespoons oil
1 teaspoon salt
1 teaspoon chilli powder
½ teaspoon ground turmeric
2 tablespoons dhana jeera (p. 8)

1 green chilli, chopped
1 teaspoon mustard seeds
a few drops of lemon or lime juice
1 tomato, sliced
1 tablespoon chopped fresh coriander

---

1. Wash the okra thoroughly, and top and tail. Wipe each okra with kitchen paper and split open on one side lengthways.

2. To prepare the stuffing, mix 1 tablespoon oil with the salt, chilli powder, turmeric, dhana jeera and chopped fresh chilli. Stuff each okra with a little of this masala.

3. Put the remaining oil in a wok or a deep frying pan. When it's hot, add the mustard seeds. As the seeds splutter, add the okra and stir-fry for 10–15 minutes until soft.

4. Sprinkle with a few drops of lemon or lime juice, decorate with the tomato slices and chopped fresh coriander, and serve.

Naan Bread (page 86), Creamy Mushroom Curry (page 57), Green Chillies Stuffed with Peanut Masala (page 98)

· PEAS IN A SPICY TOMATO SAUCE ·

There is nothing like fresh peas to bring out the true flavour of this curry but, as a substitute, frozen peas will suffice (some supermarkets now stock fresh shelled peas in chilled compartments). Serve this curry hot, with Puris (p. 82) or rice.

―――――――――――――― SERVES 2 ――――――――――――――

1 tablespoon oil
½ teaspoon mustard seeds
½ teaspoon cumin seeds
½ teaspoon asafoetida
225g (8oz) shelled peas
3 big tomatoes, skinned (p. 4) and cut into cubes

1 teaspoon salt
1 teaspoon chilli powder
¼ teaspoon ground turmeric
1 tablespoon dhana jeera (p. 8)
1 teaspoon sugar
½ teaspoon lemon or lime juice

1. Heat the oil in a saucepan. When it's hot, add the mustard and cumin seeds. As the seeds splutter add the asafoetida and peas. Stir-fry for 2–3 minutes. Add 175ml (6fl oz) water and let it simmer for 5 minutes, until the peas have softened a little.

2. Add the chopped tomatoes, salt, chilli powder, turmeric, dhana jeera and sugar. Cover and cook for a further 15 minutes, until the curry is thick.

3. Add the lemon or lime juice and serve.

Potato & Stuffed Baby
· Aubergine Curry ·

My version of this recipe is quick and retains the delicate flavour of the baby aubergines. If long, thin baby aubergines are not available, use a large aubergine cut into finger-sized pieces.

Serves 4

6 small potatoes, boiled and peeled
1½ teaspoons salt
1 teaspoon chilli powder
½ teaspoon ground turmeric
2 tablespoons dhana jeera (p. 8)
1 tablespoon tomato purée
4 tablespoons oil

6–8 baby aubergines or 1 large
   aubergine
1 teaspoon cumin seeds
½ teaspoon mustard seeds
1 teaspoon grated fresh ginger
1 green chilli, de-seeded and finely
   chopped
chopped fresh coriander

---

1. Cut the boiled potatoes into large cubes. (If using new potatoes, just cut them in half and do not peel.)

2. Mix the salt, chilli powder, turmeric, dhana jeera, tomato purée and 2 tablespoons oil in a small bowl.

3. Cut the aubergines lengthways into 4 sections held together at the stalk. Stuff each aubergine with the spice mixture, reserving any leftover mixture. If using a large aubergine, cut each finger-sized piece in half, three-quarters of the way down their length, and then stuff with the spice mixture.

4. Heat the remaining oil in a large saucepan. When it's hot, add the cumin and mustard seeds. As soon as they start to pop, add the ginger and aubergines. Cover and cook over a medium heat for 5 minutes.

5. Add the green chilli, potatoes, any remaining spice mixture and 300ml (10fl oz) water. Cover and cook for 15–20 minutes, stirring from time to time, until tender. Serve garnished with the chopped fresh coriander.

· MATTAR PANEER ·

Paneer is fresh unripened cheese, made by curdling the milk with a souring agent (yogurt and lemon in this case); it is similar to ricotta cheese.

This spicy Mogul dish tastes best if you use freshly prepared paneer, which is quite straightforward to make. The recipe below makes 175g (6oz) paneer. If you are very pressed for time you can use bought paneer (which needs to be cut into cubes and added to the curry) but freshly made paneer tastes better in this recipe.

———————————— SERVES 6 ————————————

PANEER
1.2 litres (2 pints) whole or semi-
   skimmed milk
2 tablespoons natural yogurt
2–3 teaspoons bottled lemon juice

CURRY
2 tablespoons oil
1 teaspoon mustard seeds
1 teaspoon cumin seeds
2 cinnamon sticks
1 dry red chilli
3 whole cloves
3 cardamom pods, split
1 large onion, peeled and chopped
a 2.5cm (1 inch) piece ginger, peeled
   and grated

2 green chillies, de-seeded and chopped
3 garlic cloves, peeled and crushed
1 teaspoon salt
1 teaspoon chilli powder
1 teaspoon garam masala (p. 9)
½ teaspoon ground turmeric
2 tablespoons dhana jeera (p. 8)
1 teaspoon sugar
2 teaspoons poppy seeds
2 tomatoes, chopped
175g (6oz) paneer
450g (1lb) frozen peas
175ml (6fl oz) whey (if collected) or
   water
4 tablespoons single cream or yoghurt
a few fresh coriander leaves

————————————————— • —————————————————

FOR THE PANEER

1. Bring the milk to boiling point in a large heavy-based saucepan, then stir in the yogurt. Reduce the heat and add the lemon juice, stirring until large soft curds form and the liquid around them becomes clear. Turn off the heat.

2. Sieve the contents of the pan, and leave the paneer to drain for 5 minutes. The whey collected can be used as a liquid stock for this curry or any other curry or soup. You can store it in the fridge for 2 days.

For the Curry

1. Meanwhile, heat the oil in a large saucepan and fry the mustard seeds, cumin seeds, cinnamon sticks, dry red chilli, cloves and cardamom pods for 2 minutes, until the seeds pop.

2. Add the onion and sauté for 5 minutes, until lightly browned, then stir in the ginger, green chillies and garlic and cook for 2 minutes.

3. Add the salt, chilli powder, garam masala, turmeric, dhana jeera, sugar and poppy seeds and stir well.

4. Add the tomatoes, paneer, peas and 175ml (6fl oz) whey or water. Simmer for 10 minutes, breaking up the paneer as it cooks until it resembles cottage cheese.

5. Stir in the cream or yogurt and serve hot, sprinkled with the fresh coriander leaves.

· STIR-FRIED AUBERGINE ·

This quick aubergine dish, using the big aubergines from Holland and Spain, has an appetising smoky flavour. Serve it with Naan (p. 86) or rice.

SERVES 2

1 large aubergine	1 teaspoon salt
1 large onion	1 teaspoon chilli powder (or less to
½ green pepper	taste)
2 tablespoons oil	½ teaspoon garam masala (p. 9)
1 teaspoon cumin seeds	2 teaspoons dhana jeera (p. 8)
1 teaspoon grated fresh ginger	½ teaspoon sugar
1 long green chilli, de-seeded and	a few fresh coriander leaves
chopped	

1. Wash the aubergine and make a couple of long slits on the outside. Either place it under a hot grill, which is quicker and easier, or bake in a hot oven at 180°C/350°F (Gas Mark 4), until it is soft and tender (about 15–20 minutes). Remove the skin (which should come off easily) and chop the aubergine into big cubes.

2. Cut half the onion into cubes and the green pepper into squares and reserve. Chop the remaining half of the onion.

3. Heat the oil in a wok or a deep frying pan. When it's hot, add the cumin seeds. As they start to darken, add the chopped onion and sauté till brown. Add the ginger, fresh chilli, aubergine, salt, chilli powder, garam masala, dhana jeera and sugar. Stir and cook for only 7–10 minutes, transfer to a serving dish and garnish with the coriander leaves.

4. In the same pan, add extra oil if necessary and quickly brown the squares of onion and green pepper. Spice this mixture with a little salt and chilli powder. Arrange it on the dish around the aubergine and serve at once.

· STIR-FRIED SPINACH ·

There are numerous ways of cooking spinach but this elegant method, where fresh spinach is lightly stir-fried in flavoured gram flour, creates a stunning green and yellow marbled effect. Serve this dish as a starter, or as part of a main meal with Cumin Potatoes (p. 28) or Sesame Potatoes (p. 29).

SERVES 4

1 × 225g (8oz) packet of spinach (or 3–4 bunches)
2 cloves garlic, peeled
2 tablespoons oil
1 teaspoon mustard seeds
1 teaspoon salt
½ teaspoon chilli powder
1 tablespoon dhana jeera (p. 8)
1 green chilli, chopped
2 tablespoons gram flour
½ teaspoon lemon or lime juice

1. First prepare the spinach. Trim the stalks and wash well, then chop or coarsely shred the leaves. Thinly slice the garlic.

2. Heat the oil in a wok or a deep frying pan. When it's hot, add the mustard seeds, garlic and spinach. Sauté for 6 minutes, until the spinach wilts. Add the salt, chilli powder, dhana jeera and fresh chilli.

3. In a small bowl mix the gram flour with 4 tablespoons water; gently pour this mixture into the wok and stir well for 5 minutes, until the spinach is well blended with the gram flour paste. Cover the pan and simmer over a medium heat for 10 minutes.

4. Season to taste with lemon or lime juice and serve at once.

· FENUGREEK DUMPLINGS ·

Fenugreek is a small-leafed Indian spinach with a slightly bitter flavour. Use it like spinach for its nutritional value. Chapaty flour is available from Asian stores.

These tasty dumplings are a very useful addition to many curries and rice dishes and they freeze well. Simply remove them from the freezer 10 minutes early to defrost. When unexpected guests arrive, adding a few of these dumplings to a simple curry can transform it into something really special. Gently add the dumplings for the last 5 minutes of cooking time. Their flavour should blend with the rest of the food but they must still stay whole.

You could serve them with a chutney as a starter if you like the bitter taste, but generally they are added to Spiced Yogurt Soup (p. 78) and served with other vegetable curries or rice dishes.

MAKES 15 SMALL DUMPLINGS

½ bunch fenugreek leaves (discard the hard stalks)
1 tablespoon fresh coriander leaves
2 tablespoons chapaty flour
2 tablespoons gram flour
½ teaspoon salt
½ teaspoon chilli powder
2 teaspoons dhana jeera (p. 8)

¼ teaspoon asafoetida
¼ teaspoon baking powder
½ teaspoon sugar
½ teaspoon chopped green chilli
2 teaspoons oil
½ teaspoon lemon juice
extra oil

1. Finely chop the fenugreek and coriander leaves.

2. Put all the above ingredients (except the extra oil) in a bowl and mix by hand, adding 1–2 tablespoons water to bind well. Divide the mixture into 15 small balls.

3. Grease your hands slightly with oil and re-roll to smooth the dumplings.

4. Heat some oil in a wok or a deep frying pan. When it's hot, add the dumplings, deep-fry till golden, and drain on kitchen paper.

· CLUSTER OR FRENCH BEAN CURRY ·

Cluster bean (guvar) curry is a familiar dish in most Gujarati households – long thin guvar resemble flat French beans and are very high in nutrients, especially iron. If guvar are not available, Kenyan French Beans can be used as a substitute.

Serve this dish as part of a main meal with any potato curry, rice and Indian bread.

SERVES 2–3

225g (8oz) cluster beans (guvar)
1 tablespoon oil
½ teaspoon mustard seeds
½ teaspoon fenugreek seeds
1 teaspoon ajwain seeds
1 teaspoon salt

1 teaspoon chilli powder
¼ teaspoon ground turmeric
1 tablespoon dhana jeera (p. 8)
1 teaspoon jaggery or brown sugar
1 small tomato (optional)

1. Top and tail the guvar. (To do this quickly, lay 8–10 guvar on a chopping board in a bundle and top and tail with a sharp knife.) Wash well. If they are long, cut them in half.

2. Heat the oil in a pan. When it's hot, add the mustard, fenugreek and ajwain seeds; let them splutter and add the guvar. Stir-fry for 3–4 minutes.

3. Add the salt, chilli powder, turmeric, dhana jeera and jaggery or brown sugar, one by one. Add 8 tablespoons water, cover and simmer for 15–20 minutes until the guvar are soft and the sauce is thick.

4. If using a tomato, cut into small cubes and add towards the last 5 minutes of cooking time.

· CURRIED DRUMSTICKS ·

The Indian name for drumsticks is saragva-ni-singh. They are very nutritious long green pods with a thick, fibrous skin and a fleshy pulp with soft seeds inside.

Cooked drumsticks are considered a great delicacy in India; their flavour is often compared with asparagus. In fact if you cannot get hold of drumsticks, you can substitute 1 bunch (15–20 spears) asparagus. Follow the recipe below but cut down on the cooking time depending on the size of the asparagus.

SERVES 4

4 long drumsticks
1 tablespoon oil
½ teaspoon mustard seeds
½ teaspoon asafoetida
2 tablespoons gram flour
1 teaspoon salt

1 teaspoon chilli powder
¼ teaspoon ground turmeric
1 teaspoon sugar
2 teaspoons dhana jeera (p. 8)
1 teaspoon lemon juice

1. Cut the drumsticks into 5cm (2 inch) pieces, giving a total of about 20 pieces. Peel off any fibrous skin that comes apart during slicing.

2. Heat the oil in a pan and add the mustard seeds and asafoetida. Add the drumsticks and sauté for 2–3 minutes. Add 175ml (6fl oz) water and cover the pan. Let it all cook for 15 minutes until the drumsticks are soft.

3. While the mixture is cooking, mix the gram flour with 4 tablespoons water in a bowl to form a smooth paste.

4. When the drumsticks are soft, lower the heat and add the gram flour paste, salt, chilli powder, turmeric, sugar and dhana jeera. Mix well and cook for about 10 minutes, until the sauce has thickened to a dipping consistency.

5. Add the lemon juice and serve warm on individual plates. This dish is eaten by sucking the inside of the pods, together with the spicy gravy, and throwing away the fibrous remains.

· PANEER & CASHEW NUT KORMA ·

The subtle flavour and colour of the coconut milk and saffron give this korma a unique taste; and it makes an eye-catching centrepiece for a dinner party. Friends will think you have spent hours cooking it, but my recipe takes less than half an hour! Serve it with Puris (p. 82), Potato and Stuffed Baby Aubergine Curry (p. 45), Lemon Rice (p. 72) and Stir-Fry Relish (p. 96), followed by Carrot Halwa (p. 107) or Semolina Halwa (p. 108).

Ready-made paneer is available from chilled compartments in super-markets and Asian grocers. (It is better to use the bought variety in this recipe.)

SERVES 4

100g (4oz) cashew nuts
100g (4oz) paneer
6–8 saffron strands
2 tablespoons oil
1 red onion or Spanish onion, peeled
   and sliced
1 teaspoon grated fresh ginger
1 green chilli, de-seeded and chopped
½ green pepper, cut into strips
1 teaspoon salt

1 teaspoon chilli powder
½ teaspoon garam masala (p. 9)
4 tablespoons tinned coconut milk or
   2 tablespoons creamed coconut
1 tablespoon Tamarind Sauce (p. 93)
1 tablespoon desiccated or fresh grated
   coconut
lemon juice to taste
a few fresh coriander leaves

---

1. Soak the cashew nuts in hot water for 10 minutes until soft, then drain. Cut the paneer into small cubes, and soak the saffron strands in 1 tablespoon water in a saucer.

2. Heat the oil in a wok or a deep frying pan and sauté the onion, ginger and chilli for 3 minutes. Add the nuts and paneer, and stir-fry for 4–5 minutes.

3. Add the green pepper and salt, chilli powder and garam masala. Stir well and add the coconut milk or creamed coconut, tamarind sauce, grated coconut and saffron water. Mix well, add 4 tablespoons water and cook, covered, for 10–12 minutes. Stir once or twice; it thickens as it cooks.

4. Add lemon juice to taste, garnish with the coriander leaves and serve hot.

· STUFFED KARELA ·

Karela is a lumpy green gourd, about 10–15cm (4–6 inches) long, available from Asian grocers. It has many nutritional properties, especially in controlling the blood sugar level. It also has a very bitter flavour which is an acquired taste. Some of the bitternss can be removed by soaking or parboiling the karela in salted water, or you could sweeten the curry with a little jaggery or brown sugar.

Serve hot as part of a main meal with any potato dish, or a dal, rice and Indian bread.

SERVES 2–3

2 karelas	½ teaspoon chilli powder
2 tablespoons oil	2 teaspoons dhana jeera (p. 8)
2 tablespoons gram flour	½ teaspoon mustard seeds
1 tablespoon peanuts, ground in a	½ teaspoon asafoetida
coffee grinder	1 small tomato, finely chopped
½ teaspoon salt	

1. Top and tail the karelas and, using a vegetable peeler, remove the green, coarse wrinkled skin. Cut into 2.5cm (1 inch) pieces and parboil in salted water for 10 minutes.

2. When cold, use a sharp knife to remove the seeds from the centre.

3. To prepare the stuffing, heat 1 tablespoon oil in a wok or a frying pan and sauté the gram flour for 4–5 minutes, until it changes colour. Add the chopped peanuts and the salt, chilli powder and dhana jeera. When cold, use a teaspoon to stuff the centre of each piece of karela with the mixture.

4. In a pan, heat 1 tablespoon oil and add the mustard seeds and asafoetida. Add the stuffed karela pieces and 2 tablespoons water and simmer covered for 5–7 minutes.

5. Garnish with the finely chopped tomato and serve hot.

—— VARIATION ——

Courgettes can be stuffed and cooked in the same way as karela to make a delicious curry. In fact I often cook the curry with a mixture of the two; the bitterness of the karela and the sweetness of the courgette seem to complement each other.

✦ Cut 2 courgettes into 2.5cm (1 inch) pieces and use a sharp knife to remove the centre section. (There is no need to parboil the courgettes.)

✦ Prepare the same stuffing mixture as above, stuff the courgette pieces and cook in the same way.

GREEN PEPPER & TOMATO
· CURRY ·

Green peppers can be a great standby. They cook quickly and their flavour goes with many vegetables. The green and red of the pepper and tomato also make this a very attractive dish. I usually add 2 tablespoons coconut milk for the last 5 minutes of the cooking time (to gain a consistency that is somewhere between a curry and a dal).

Serve this dish with any dry curry, such as Stir-Fried Okra (p. 42) or Potato and Cauliflower Curry (p. 39), Puris (p. 82) or Parathas (p. 88) and rice.

SERVES 2

1 big green pepper
225g (8oz) tomatoes
2 tablespoons oil
1 teaspoon cumin seeds
1 teaspoon salt
1 teaspoon chilli powder
¼ teaspoon ground turmeric

1 tablespoon dhana jeera (p. 8)
½ teaspoon garam masala (p. 9)
1 teaspoon jaggery or brown sugar
2 tablespoons tinned coconut milk
  (optional)
lemon juice
a few fresh coriander leaves

1. Wash and de-seed the green pepper and cut it into big chunks. Cut the tomatoes into equal-sized chunks.

2. Heat the oil in a wok or a deep frying pan. When it's hot, add the cumin seeds and green pepper. Sauté for 2–3 minutes and add the tomatoes. Cook for 5 minutes.

3. Add the salt, chilli powder, turmeric, dhana jeera, garam masala and jaggery or brown sugar, one by one. Simmer covered, for 7 minutes, adding the coconut milk for the last 5 minutes if you wish.

4. Season to taste with the lemon juice, garnish with the coriander leaves and serve.

· CREAMY MUSHROOM CURRY ·

This mushroom curry has been appreciated by most of my students. It works well as part of a Western or Eastern dinner party and it can be cooked at any time of the year because of the constant availability of fresh mushrooms. To keep their delicate flavour, take care not to overcook the mushrooms.

SERVES 4

450g (1lb) mushrooms (button or flat)
3 tablespoons oil
1 onion, peeled and chopped
1 teaspoon grated fresh ginger
1 teaspoon chopped green chilli
1 teaspoon salt
1 teaspoon chilli powder
¼ teaspoon ground turmeric
2 tablespoons dhana jeera (p. 8)

½ teaspoon garam masala (p. 9)
½ teaspoon tandoori masala
2 fresh tomatoes or 2 tablespoons
    tinned tomatoes, chopped
1 teaspoon sugar (optional)
1 teaspoon lemon juice (optional)
2–3 tablespoons single cream or yogurt
a few fresh coriander leaves

1. Wash or wipe the mushrooms. Keep the small ones whole and cut the big ones into 2–4 pieces.

2. In a big pan, heat the oil and sauté the chopped onion. When brown, add the ginger and fresh chilli. Remove from the oil with a slotted spoon and set aside.

3. Add the mushrooms to the same pan and sauté for 4–5 minutes. Add the salt, chilli powder, turmeric, dhana jeera, garam masala and tandoori masala, and stir well. Add the chopped tomatoes and the onion mixture, cover and cook for 8–10 minutes.

4. Add the sugar and lemon juice only if desired.

5. Just before serving, mix in the cream or yogurt and garnish with the coriander leaves.

SWEETCORN IN A SPICY
· PEANUT SAUCE ·

This is a quick nourishing curry, full of protein, a great party dish.

Instead of sweetcorn kernels, you can use fresh whole corn-on-the-cob, cut into bite-size pieces and parboiled. You can also use salted peanuts but remember to use less salt for the curry.

SERVES 4

1 tablespoon oil
1 teaspoon cumin seeds
1 big onion, peeled and chopped
1 teaspoon grated fresh ginger
1 green chilli, de-seeded and chopped
4 tablespoons fresh skinned tomatoes (p. 4) or tinned tomatoes, chopped
1 teaspoon salt

1 teaspoon chilli powder
2 teaspoons dhana jeera (p. 8)
½ teaspoon garam masala (p. 9)
a pinch of ground turmeric
350g (12oz) frozen or tinned sweetcorn
4 tablespoons chopped unsalted peanuts
1 teaspoon lemon juice
some chopped fresh coriander or red chilli

1. Heat the oil in a large saucepan. When it's hot, add the cumin seeds and sauté the chopped onion till golden.

2. Add the ginger, fresh chilli, tomatoes, salt, chilli powder, dhana jeera, garam masala and turmeric, and cook for 2–3 minutes.

3. Add the sweetcorn, 4–6 tablespoons water, and the chopped peanuts, and cook for a further 15 minutes.

4. Mix the curry well, add the lemon juice, garnish with the chopped fresh coriander or chilli and serve.

OPPOSITE, CLOCKWISE FROM TOP OF PLATE: Stir-Fry Relish (page 96), Saffron Rice (page 71), Masala-Spiced Sugar Snap Peas and Cashew Nuts (page 25)

OPPOSITE PAGE 59, CLOCKWISE FROM TOP: Black-Eye Bean Curry (in bowl, page 64), Sweetcorn in a Spicy Peanut Sauce (above), Boiled Rice with Fennel Seeds (page 70), Red Onion Relish (page 100)

CHAPTER FOUR

PULSES

Aꜱ ᴛʜᴇ ɴᴀᴍᴇ suggests, pulses (dry peas, beans and lentils) are really the 'heart' of a vegetarian diet. All pulses are a good source of high-quality protein, carbohydrates, vitamins, minerals (especially iron) and soluble fibre.

Pulses are rich in lysine, which is one of the essential amino acids. But to get 'complete protein', it's best to combine them with grains and nuts. Indian cuisine naturally solves this problem, for bean and lentil curries are always eaten with grains (puris, parathas or rice) to provide a balanced intake of protein.

Dal is a Sanskrit word meaning 'to divide or split', which is the treatment that the lentils, peas and beans undergo, so the dishes using split pulses are called 'dal'.

Many people are put off eating pulses because of their reputation for causing flatulence. However the spices used in Indian cooking, especially asafoetida, cumin, coriander and ginger, all help to aid digestion. You can also reduce the problem by gradually increasing your regular intake of beans so that the body gets used to the extra roughage. Sprouted beans do not cause flatulence because the starch is partially converted to sugar.

These days a wide variety of very high-quality tinned pulses are available in supermarkets. For a quick meal these tins are ideal, as they save on all the cooking and soaking time. If you prefer to use dried pulses, see the tips below.

There is only one recipe in this chapter that is not suitable for a vegan diet – Spiced Sprouting Bean Salad on page 68.

TIPS ON COOKING PULSES

1. Pulses soaked overnight cook faster and more evenly.

2. Never cook pulses in their soaking water, as it contains some of the indigestible sugars.

3. When using dried pulses, try to cook them in a wide, heavy-bottom saucepan to minimise the cooking time.

· CHANA DAL ·

This is the yellow mushy dal served in Indian restaurants to accompany curries and rice. It is easy to prepare and the mild nutty flavour goes well with any other hot curries. Serve it with Puris (p. 82) and rice.

Chana dal is the husked dal of small dark chickpeas; it is stocked by most supermarkets.

SERVES 4

100g (4oz) chana dal
2 tablespoons oil
2 cinnamon sticks
1 dry red chilli
1 small onion, peeled and finely
  shredded
a 2.5cm (1 inch) piece of fresh ginger,
  peeled and grated
1 green chilli, de-seeded and chopped
2 fresh tomatoes or 2 tablespoons
  tinned tomatoes, chopped

1 teaspoon salt (or more to taste)
½ teaspoon chilli powder
¼ teaspoon ground turmeric
1 teaspoon tandoori masala (powder
  rather than paste)
1 teaspoon sugar
1 teaspoon lemon juice (optional)
1 tablespoon fresh coriander leaves

1. Wash the chana dal well and cook it in plenty of unsalted water until it is soft when touched between two fingers (about 15–20 minutes) or steam in a pressure cooker for 10 minutes.

2. Heat the oil in a wok or deep frying pan. When it's hot, add the cinnamon sticks and the dry red chilli, and sauté the onion.

3. Add the ginger, green chilli and tomatoes. Then stir in the salt, chilli powder, turmeric, tandoori masala and sugar. Add the soft dal, mix well and simmer for 10 minutes.

4. A little lemon juice will give it a sharper taste if desired. Garnish with the fresh coriander leaves and serve.

· YELLOW MOONG BEAN CURRY ·

The subtle yellow colour of this curry, garnished with red chilli and coriander, makes it a colourful addition to any meal.

Husked moong beans are the Gujarati Jains' favourite lentils. Jains are a strict vegetarian sect. *Ahimsa* (non-violence) is their main path to Nirvana. Some Jains fast on religious days or eat a very simple diet to minimise the taking of life; in the process they are trying to conserve the environment.

SERVES 4

175g (6oz) husked, yellow, split moong beans
2 tablespoons oil
½ teaspoon mustard seeds
½ teaspoon cumin seeds
1 teaspoon salt
1 teaspoon sugar

1 teaspoon chilli powder
¼ teaspoon ground turmeric
¼ teaspoon asafoetida
1 teaspoon lemon or lime juice
a long green or red chilli
a few fresh coriander leaves

1. Wash the moong beans thoroughly, soak them for 10 minutes, then drain well.

2. Heat the oil in a pan, and add the mustard and cumin seeds. When the seeds splutter, add the moong beans and 225ml (8fl oz) water. Bring to the boil and simmer gently for 10 minutes. Use a spoon to remove any froth that rises to the surface.

3. Add the salt, sugar, chilli powder, turmeric and asafoetida, and simmer, covered, for a few minutes until the beans are soft but still moist and whole.

4. Add the lemon or lime juice, garnish with the chilli and coriander, and serve at once.

· GREEN MOONG BEAN CURRY ·

This simple dish makes use of the widely available whole, green moong beans which are easy to cook and digest. The curry goes well with plain rice, Sweet Puris (p. 83), Puris (p. 82) or Naan (p. 86).

SERVES 4

100g (4oz) moong beans
1 tablespoon oil
½ teaspoon mustard seeds
1 teaspoon cumin seeds
½ teaspoon asafoetida
a 1.5cm (½ inch) piece of fresh ginger,
    peeled and grated
1 big tomato, chopped

1 teaspoon salt
½ teaspoon chilli powder
½ teaspoon garam masala (p. 9)
½ teaspoon ground turmeric
1 tablespoon dhana jeera (p. 8)
1 teaspoon jaggery or brown sugar
1 teaspoon lemon juice
a few fresh coriander leaves

1. Wash the moong beans and either pressure-cook them in 600ml (1 pint) water for 10 minutes, or boil them in a pan for 20 minutes or more, till very soft. Add extra water if required.

2. Meanwhile, heat the oil in another saucepan and add the mustard seeds, cumin seeds and asafoetida. When the seeds splutter, add the ginger, tomato, salt, chilli powder, garam masala, turmeric, dhana jeera and jaggery or brown sugar. Cook and stir for 2 minutes.

3. When the moong beans are soft, add the beans and their cooking liquid to the saucepan with the spiced oil. Mix everything well, cover the pan and simmer till the curry is thick (about 10–15 minutes).

4. Season with the lemon juice, garnish with the coriander leaves and serve.

· BLACK-EYE BEAN CURRY ·

Tinned black-eye beans are very handy to use. They are available from most supermarkets and the curry can be ready to eat in a very short time. Serve it with other curries and Puris (p. 82) or Parathas (p. 88).

SERVES 4

1 × 400g (14oz) tin black-eye beans
2 tablespoons oil
½ teaspoon mustard seeds
½ teaspoon cumin seeds
½ teaspoon asafoetida
1 teaspoon grated fresh ginger
1 tablespoon gram flour
½ green pepper, cut into strips
3–4 tomatoes or 3 tablespoons tinned
    tomatoes, chopped

1 teaspoon salt (or more to taste)
1 teaspoon chilli powder
¼ teaspoon ground turmeric
1 tablespoon dhana jeera (p. 8)
½ teaspoon garam masala (p. 9)
1 teaspoon sugar
1 teaspoon lemon juice
1 tablespoon chopped spring onions

1. Open the tin of black-eye beans and rinse the beans in cold water to get rid of the thick liquid that sticks to them.

2. Heat the oil in a pan over a medium heat. Add the mustard seeds, cumin seeds, asafoetida, ginger and gram flour. Stir for 2 minutes, then add the green pepper, tomatoes, salt, chilli powder, turmeric, dhana jeera, garam masala and sugar, one by one. Cook for 3 minutes.

3. Add the black-eye beans and 175ml (6 fl oz) water to the pan, mix well, cover and simmer for 10 minutes.

4. Add the lemon juice and garnish with the spring onions before serving.

· MIXED DAL WITH FRESH SPINACH ·

This dal dish is like a thick, yellow soup with greens floating in it – very healthy and delicious. It's excellent with bread or rice.

SERVES 2–4

1 tablespoon orange-yellow tuvar dal
1 tablespoon chana dal
1 tablespoon husked yellow moong dal
1 tablespoon orange masoor dal
1 teaspoon salt
1 teaspoon chilli powder
¼ teaspoon ground turmeric
1 teaspoon lemon juice

1 long green chilli, de-seeded and cut
   into small circles
50g (2oz) fresh spinach
2 tablespoons oil
½ teaspoon mustard seeds
½ Spanish onion, peeled and finely
   shredded
2 garlic cloves, peeled and sliced

1. Mix all 4 dals or any other combination of dals you prefer. Wash well, soak for 10 minutes in hot water, and drain.

2. Pressure-cook in 600ml (1 pint) water for 15 minutes, or longer (about 30 minutes) in an ordinary pan, until the dal mixture is very soft. (Add extra water if needed.)

3. Add the salt, chilli powder, turmeric, lemon juice and green chilli. Tear the spinach into large pieces and add it to the mixture.

4. Heat the oil in a pan, add the mustard seeds and sauté the finely shredded onion till brown. Add the garlic, sizzle the whole mixture and, just before serving, pour this flavoured hot oil over the dal.

· SPICY CHICKPEAS AND SPINACH ·

Another variation using tinned chickpeas is with frozen spinach and spices. This dish is quick, nutritious and tasty. Serve it with Bhatura (p. 87) or rice or as part of a main meal. The amchoor (dried, powdered mango) adds a little extra sourness but it's not essential.

SERVES 4

1 × 400g (14oz) tin chickpeas
1 tablespoon oil
½ teaspoon cumin seeds
½ teaspoon asafoetida
½ Spanish onion, peeled and chopped
½ green pepper (optional), de-seeded and sliced
3–4 tablespoons frozen spinach

3 tablespoons tinned chopped tomatoes or 2 big fresh tomatoes, finely chopped
1 teaspoon salt (or more to taste)
1 teaspoon chilli powder
1 tablespoon dhana jeera (p. 8)
1 teaspoon amchoor (optional)
1 teaspoon sugar
1 tablespoon Tamarind Sauce (p. 93) or lime juice

1. Rinse the chickpeas under cold water.

2. Heat the oil in a pan and add the cumin and asafoetida. Sauté the onion in this oil until it's brown. Add the green pepper if using, the spinach and tomato, and stir for 3 minutes.

3. Add the salt, chilli powder, dhana jeera, amchoor if using, and sugar, one at a time, and the tamarind sauce or lime juice.

4. Stir in the chickpeas and 175ml (6fl oz) water, season to taste, cover and cook for 10 more minutes. It's ready when the thick green sauce sticks to the chickpeas.

· SWEETCORN & KIDNEY BEAN CURRY ·

This is one of the quickest, most nourishing and substantial curries you can prepare. The ginger, garlic, cumin and asafoetida make it easier to digest the excellent protein and carbohydrate found in the kidney beans.

Serve this curry with Naan (p. 86) or rice.

SERVES 6
---

1 × 400g (14oz) tin kidney beans
1 × 350g (12oz) tin sweetcorn
2 tablespoons oil
1 teaspoon cumin seeds
½ teaspoon asafoetida
1 small onion or ½ Spanish onion, peeled and chopped
1–2 garlic cloves, peeled and crushed
1 teaspoon grated fresh ginger

1 green chilli, de-seeded and chopped
3 fresh tomatoes, skinned (p. 4) and chopped, or 3 tablespoons tinned chopped tomatoes
1 teaspoon salt
1 teaspoon chilli powder
1 tablespoon dhana jeera (p. 8)
175ml (6fl oz) tinned coconut milk (optional)

1. Rinse the kidney beans and sweetcorn under cold water.

2. Heat the oil in a pan and add the cumin seeds and asafoetida. Sauté the onion in this oil until it's brown.

3. Add the garlic, ginger and chilli and stir for 2 minutes. Mix in the tomatoes and the salt, chilli powder and dhana jeera.

4. Stir in the sweetcorn and the kidney beans. Add the coconut milk (you can add 175ml (6fl oz) water instead if you are not fond of coconut milk), cover the pan and let it simmer for 15 minutes.

· SPICED SPROUTING BEAN SALAD ·

Packets of sprouting bean salad – a mixture of chickpeas, adzuki beans, moong beans, and lentil sprouts – are now available in many supermarkets. This recipe is based on the bought mixture but, if you prefer, you can use any combination of bean sprouts or even sprout your own.

Sprouted beans are very nutritious, and this lightly spiced salad is a favourite with all my students. Serve it as a starter, or as a side dish with any selection of curries, rice and dal.

SERVES 2

1 tablespoon oil
½ teaspoon mustard seeds
1 teaspoon cumin seeds
1 teaspoon grated fresh ginger
1 green chilli, de-seeded and finely chopped
150g (5oz) sprouted beans

1 teaspoon salt
½ teaspoon chilli powder
1 teaspoon lemon or lime juice
2–3 tablespoons yogurt
a few mixed lettuce and chicory leaves

1. Heat the oil in a wok or a deep frying pan and add the mustard and cumin seeds. When the seeds pop, mix in the ginger, green chilli and sprouted beans.

2. Add the salt and chilli powder and flavour with lemon or lime juice. Cook for no longer than 5–8 minutes.

3. When cold (after about 10 minutes), mix with the yogurt and serve on a bed of mixed lettuce and chicory.

— CHAPTER FIVE —

RICE DISHES

An Indian meal revolves around rice, which is the staple food of India. Rice plays a significant role in all Hindu religious rituals and it is used in wedding ceremonies as a symbol of fertility.

Rice can be mixed with a wide range of vegetables, pulses and grains to make starters, snacks, main courses or desserts. In fact, plain rice has been compared to a blank canvas on which the colourful spices and vegetables can be painted to give a new picture each time (the rice takes on a new flavour with each recipe).

Rice is easy to digest, so it is an ideal food for children. And anyone suffering from ill-health will benefit from eating rice with milk or yoghurt. (The water that the rice is cooked in is excellent for stopping diarrhoea.)

If you use Basmati, the best-quality rice, and follow the instructions in these recipes, I am sure you will achieve fluffy, separate grains of rice every time.

The only recipes in this chapter that are not suitable for serving to vegans are those on pages 76, 78–9 and 60.

· BOILED RICE ·

There are many different ways of cooking rice, but this is the method I use to get perfect, white, fluffy rice with every grain separate. Following these instructions, even a beginner can manage to cook perfect rice.

SERVES 2

---

6 tablespoons Basmati rice

1 teaspoon fennel seeds (optional)

---

1. Wash the rice in cold water 3–4 times to remove the starch. Then soak in cold water for 10 minutes.

2. Meanwhile, boil 1.2 litres (2 pints) water in a large pan. Drain the rice and add it to the boiling water. (Never touch or wash rice that has been soaking – it is delicate and brittle.)

3. Cook, uncovered, for 12–14 minutes, until you see a little scum or froth forming on the surface. With a spoon, remove a few grains of rice, feel them between your fingers, and if they are soft to touch, remove the pan from the heat.

4. Drain off the excess water and transfer the rice to a serving dish.

5. For that special touch, add the fennel seeds to the hot cooked rice. The delicate aroma of fennel will slowly perfume the rice.

· SAFFRON RICE ·

Plain boiled rice can be transformed into the most fragrant, eye-catching dish in a few minutes.

SERVES 4–6

225g (8oz) Basmati rice
1 teaspoon saffron strands
2–3 tablespoons oil
50g (2oz) cashew or pistachio nuts
1 large onion, peeled and thinly sliced
2 dry red chillies

2–3 bay leaves
2–3 cinnamon sticks
3 cardamom pods, split open
1 teaspoon cumin seeds
1 tablespoon frozen peas, thawed
1 teaspoon salt

1. Wash the rice under cold running water for several minutes and drain well. Soak the saffron strands in 1 tablespoon warm water.

2. Cook the rice in a large pan of boiling water for 10 minutes, until just tender. Drain well and spread out on a large tray to go cold (about 10 minutes). Rice is too sticky to stir-fry when it has just been cooked, so it is best to let it get cold first.

3. Meanwhile, heat the oil in a wok or a deep frying pan, and stir-fry the nuts for 2–3 minutes until golden. Remove with a slotted spoon and set aside.

4. Add the onion to the same pan and fry until crisp and golden. Drain on kitchen paper and set aside.

5. Add a little more oil to the pan if necessary and stir-fry the chillies, bay leaves, cinnamon sticks, cardamom pods and cumin seeds. Then add the peas, cooked rice, soaked saffron with its liquid, and salt. Stir well to coat all the grains thoroughly and heat through.

6. Transfer to a large serving dish and garnish with the onion and cashew or pistachio nuts.

· LEMON RICE ·

This sparkling white rice and coconut dish has a very appetising, subtle, sharp blend of lemon juice, curry leaves and a few spices.

Urid (or urad) dal, used here for seasoning, is the small, husked, white, split lentil available from Asian stores. When it is stir-fried in oil, it gains a nutty flavour.

SERVES 4

2 tablespoons desiccated or fresh grated
  coconut
6 tablespoons Basmati rice
2 teaspoons urid dal (optional)
2 tablespoons oil
6 curry leaves

½ teaspoon mustard seeds
1 dry red chilli
1 tablespoon cashew nuts
1 teaspoon salt
juice of 1 whole lemon or lime

1. Cut open a coconut (p. 2). If there is any water, use it to cook the rice in. Peel away the thin brown skin and chop the white flesh in a food processor or grate it using a hand grater.

2. Wash the rice in cold water, then let it soak for 10 minutes. Soak the urid dal in a small bowl of cold water for 10 minutes.

3. Boil the rice in a large pan until just tender. Drain well and spread out on a large tray to go cold (about 10 minutes). Rice is too sticky to stir-fry when it has just been cooked, so it is best to let it get cold first.

4. Heat the oil in a wok or a deep frying pan and add the curry leaves, mustard seeds, dry red chilli and cashew nuts. Drain the urid dal and add to the oil, stir-fry and let everything sizzle for a few minutes.

5. Lower the heat and stir in the coconut. Add the rice, salt and lemon juice. Mix well and serve on a platter.

· SPICY PUFFED RICE ·

Puffed rice, called pawa, is a popular alternative to rice. Pawa is already cooked, pressed and dried, so it only needs to cook for a very short time. It is available from Asian stores. This dish tastes excellent with plain yogurt.

SERVES 4

175g (6oz) medium pawa
2 tablespoons oil
1–2 tablespoons cashew nuts or peanuts
1 teaspoon cumin seeds
1 potato, peeled and cut into small cubes
3 tablespoons tinned or frozen sweetcorn

1 green chilli, de-seeded and finely chopped
1 teaspoon salt
¼ teaspoon ground turmeric
1 teaspoon chilli powder
½ teaspoon garam masala (p. 9)
½ teaspoon sugar
1 teaspoon lemon juice
1 tablespoon fresh chopped coriander

1. Wash the pawa in plenty of cold water, soak for 4 minutes and drain the water. Fluff the pawa with a fork.

2. Heat the oil in a wok or a deep frying pan and gently sauté the cashew nuts or peanuts until brown. Remove and set on one side.

3. Add the cumin seeds to the same oil, and sauté the potato cubes for 5–8 minutes until soft. Add the sweetcorn, green chilli, salt, turmeric, chilli powder, garam masala and sugar. Mix well. Add the pawa and cook for 5 minutes.

4. Add the lemon juice and, just before serving, mix in the nuts and garnish with the coriander.

· AUBERGINE & GREEN LENTIL PULLAV ·

This is an unusual way of combining cooked rice with vegetables and green lentils; a great party dish appreciated by everyone. Pullav is another word for pullao or pilaff.

Serve it with Avocado and Tomato Raita (p. 103) for a light lunch or as part of a main meal with Naan (p. 86), Chana Dal (p. 61) and Creamy Mushroom Curry (p. 57) or any combination of your choice.

SERVES 4

4 tablespoons Basmati rice
4–5 fresh tomatoes or 175ml (6fl oz)
   tomato juice
3–4 tablespoons oil
100g (4oz) aubergine, cut into
   1cm (½ inch) thick slices

2 tablespoons green lentils, washed
a bunch of spring onions, finely sliced
2 teaspoons garam masala (p. 9)
1 teaspoon salt (or more to taste)
2 long green chillies, thinly sliced
   (optional)

1. Wash and soak the rice for 10 minutes. Boil for about 10 minutes, until *al dente*, and let it cool on a tray for 10 minutes.

2. If using fresh tomatoes, liquidise them and strain the juice.

3. While the rice is cooking, heat 3 tablespoons oil in a wok or deep frying pan, sauté the aubergine slices until soft and reserve on a tray. Add a little extra oil if required, and sauté the green lentils and spring onions for 5 minutes.

4. Add the freshly made or bought tomato juice to the pan, together with 125ml (4fl oz) water, and cook for 15 minutes, until the lentils are soft.

5. To this, add the aubergine slices, garam masala and salt to taste, mixing well. Stir the rice in gently, decorate with the thinly sliced green chillies if using, and serve.

· CORIANDER PULLAV ·

This aromatic rice pullav or pullao also makes a good party dish.

SERVES 4
---

6 tablespoons rice
1 tablespoon oil
2 cloves
2 cardamom pods, slightly bruised to
  release their aroma
1–2 cinnamon sticks
2–4 bay leaves
1 teaspoon cumin seeds
1 teaspoon fennel seeds
2 spring onions or 1 shallot, chopped

1 tablespoon fresh or frozen peas
1 tablespoon finely chopped French
  beans (optional)
1 tablespoon Coriander Chutney (p. 92)
  or 2 tablespoons fresh coriander
  leaves, 1 de-seeded green chilli, a
  1 cm (½ inch) piece of fresh ginger,
  and a little salt, sugar and lemon juice
1 teaspoon salt
a few pistachio nuts (optional)

---

1. Wash the rice and let it soak in cold water for 10 minutes. If you don't have any prepared coriander chutney, mix the coriander, chilli and ginger with a little salt, sugar and lemon juice in a food processor to form a paste.

2. Heat the oil in a wok or deep frying pan, add the cloves, cardamom, cinnamon, bay leaves, cumin and fennel seeds, and stir-fry for 1 minute. Add the chopped spring onions or shallot, and the peas, beans if using, and drained rice (no water at this stage), and fry for 3 minutes.

3. Stir in the coriander chutney, salt and 225–300ml (8–10fl oz) water, cover and simmer for 12–15 minutes until the rice is tender.

4. Serve on a large platter, and decorate with pistachio nuts for a special occasion.

· MASALA KHICHADI ·

Khichadi is a traditional dish in which equal amounts of rice, either Basmati or Patna, and split green moong lentils are used. It is a well-balanced, simple, easily digested meal. It was khichadi which inspired the famous breakfast dish of the Raj, kedgeree. To make it more substantial, they added eggs and fish.

This version of khichadi uses Basmati rice and husked yellow moong beans. You can serve it cold with some natural yogurt or hot with Spiced Yogurt Soup (p. 78).

─────────────── SERVES 2 ───────────────

50g (2oz) Basmati rice
50g (2oz) husked yellow moong beans
1 tablespoon butter
4 spring onions, chopped
1 teaspoon cumin seeds
6 curry leaves (optional)

2 cinnamon sticks
1 teaspoon salt
¼ teaspoon ground turmeric
1 teaspoon garam masala (p. 9)
1 tablespoon desiccated or fresh grated
  coconut (optional)

1. Wash the rice and moong beans separately in cold water.

2. Melt the butter in a wok or a deep frying pan. Add the spring onions, cumin, curry leaves if using, and cinnamon sticks, and sauté for 3 minutes. Add the rice and moong beans, and sauté for a further 3 minutes.

3. Add the salt, turmeric, garam masala and 225–300ml (8–10fl oz) water, cover and cook for 15–20 minutes until the khichadi is soft.

4. Garnish with the coconut if using, and serve.

· STIR-FRIED RICE WITH PEAS ·

Plain left-over rice can be made into a number of exciting dishes. My children's favourite is stir-fried rice with peas. Serve hot or cold with some natural yogurt.

SERVES 2

1 tablespoon oil
½ teaspoon mustard seeds
¼ teaspoon asafoetida
1 tablespoon frozen peas
6 tablespoons cooked rice (cold)

½ teaspoon salt
½ teaspoon chilli powder
¼ teaspoon ground turmeric
lemon juice
fresh coriander leaves

1. Heat the oil in a wok or deep frying pan and add the mustard seeds. When the seeds pop, add the asafoetida and peas. Stir-fry for 2–3 minutes, then add the rice, salt, chilli powder, turmeric and lemon juice.

2. Continue cooking and mixing for a further 5 minutes. Garnish with the coriander leaves and serve.

· SPICED YOGURT SOUP ·

This yogurt soup recipe is included in the rice section as it is a perfect counterpart to any rice dish. Light yellow in colour, spiced with just a few herbs, it has a very subtle flavour.

Use natural yogurt made from whole or semi–skimmed milk and serve hot with Masala Khichadi (p. 76), or any rice dish or as a soup.

SERVES 4

225ml (8fl oz) yogurt
1 tablespoon gram flour
1 tablespoon oil
2 cinnamon sticks
1 dry red chilli
8–10 curry leaves
½ teaspoon mustard seeds
½ teaspoon fenugreek seeds
1 teaspoon cumin seeds

1 teaspoon coriander seeds, slightly crushed
1 teaspoon grated fresh ginger
1 whole long green chilli
1 teaspoon salt
½ teaspoon ground turmeric
½ teaspoon garam masala (p. 9)
1 teaspoon jaggery or brown sugar
a few fresh coriander leaves

1. Put the yogurt and gram flour in a bowl with 600ml (1 pint) water. Mix with an electric mixer or a whisk and sieve the liquid through a fine nylon or metal sieve. (Discard the contents of the sieve.)

2. Heat the oil in a large pan. When it's hot, add the cinnamon sticks, dry red chilli, curry leaves, mustard, fenugreek, cumin and coriander seeds. When the seeds splutter, add the ginger and green chilli. Cook for 1 minute and gently add the strained yogurt mixture. Add the salt, turmeric, garam masala, and jaggery or brown sugar, and let it boil. As the liquid rises, stir a few times to stop the yogurt and water separating.

3. Simmer, uncovered, for 15 minutes, garnish with coriander leaves, and serve with the curry leaves, red chilli and cinnamon sticks floating in the soup. (They are only there for flavour and decoration and are not meant to be eaten!)

—— VARIATIONS ——

Yogurt Soup with Pasta Shells

This pasta and yogurt soup is a terrific way of making a quick and substantial meal. Take care to allow just enough time for the pasta to cook. If the soup is left standing, the pasta will become swollen and soggy and the amount of liquid in the soup will be correspondingly reduced.

✦ Make the Spiced Yogurt Soup as opposite.

✦ Add 75g (3oz) pasta shells (e.g. farfalle or conchiglie) for the last 10 minutes of cooking time and serve at once.

Yogurt Soup with Fenugreek Dumplings

The mild taste of creamy yogurt soup and the bitter taste of fenugreek dumplings make a great combination – the flavours balance each other, resulting in a mouthwatering dish. Serve as a starter, or with breads or with any of the rice dishes.

✦ Add 6–8 Fenugreek Dumplings (p. 50) to the yogurt soup in the last 5 minutes of cooking (enough time for them to get soft).

Yogurt Soup with Pappadums

Small pieces of pappadum, floating in yogurt soup, give it a touch of class.

✦ Use a pair of scissors to cut 2 plain pappadums into small pieces; add to the yogurt soup for the last 5 minutes of cooking time and serve in individual bowls.

· SPICED RICE PARATHAS ·

Another good standby dish combines leftover rice with chapaty flour. These spiced rice parathas taste delicious. Serve them with Mint Chutney (p. 92) or Apple and Mango Chutney (p. 99) or any shop-bought sweet mango pickle.

———— MAKES 8 RICE PARATHAS ————

4 tablespoons cooked rice (cold)
6 tablespoons chapaty flour
2 tablespoons gram flour
1 tablespoon oil
1 tablespoon yogurt
a 2.5cm (1 inch) piece of fresh ginger, grated (optional)

1 green chilli, chopped
1 tablespoon fresh chopped coriander
1 teaspoon salt
1 teaspoon chilli powder
2 teaspoons sesame seeds
½ teaspoon ground turmeric
extra oil

1. Put all the ingredients except the extra oil in a bowl and mix by hand to form a stiff dough (adding water only if necessary).

2. Divide this dough into 8 balls and roll each into a flat pancake, 10cm (4 inches) in diameter; use a little flour to help in rolling.

3. Heat a griddle or a frying pan, add 1 teaspoon oil and brown each paratha on one side for about 2 minutes, turn over, add a little more oil and cook on the other side for another 2 minutes. The parathas should be crisp on the outside but soft in the middle.

Chapter Six

Breads

Breads, made from grains, form the bulk of an Indian meal and the ancient holy books make reference to Anna (grains) and Anna Lakshmi (goddess of prosperity) as the source of life.

Grains are rich in complex carbohydrates, protein, vitamins, minerals and fibre but they lack one of the essential amino acids, so combine them with pulses, nuts and dairy products to achieve a balanced diet.

This chapter includes bread recipes using millet and maize, as well as wheat flour. All flours have a long shelf-life and are available in most supermarkets. Chapaty flour comes in many grades; I use medium for Puris and Parathas.

For deep-fried breads, such as Puris and Bhatura, use a deep frying pan, a wok or a karahi and heat the oil until a piece of bread browns in 30 seconds. Gently drop in the Indian bread, let it brown on one side, turn it over with a slotted spoon, and brown it on the other side. Lift it out and drain on a plate lined with kitchen paper before serving.

Puris, Parathas and Sweet Puris, if left over, can be eaten the next day. Serve them cold or warm them under a hot grill or in the oven.

All the recipes in this chapter can be enjoyed by vegans, apart from those on pages 85, 86, 87 and 90.

· PURIS ·

Chapaty is the popular bread cooked in most Indian households, but preparing it requires patience and skill. Daughters are taught by their mothers to roll chapaty as soon as they can handle a rolling pin; and, throughout their lives, they perfect the art of chapaty-rolling.

Chapaty are thin, round breads, roasted at the right temperature, spread with a little smear of ghee or butter; and used as a scoop to eat spicy curries.

I always recommend that anyone attempting to cook Indian breads for the first time should start with puris, which are smaller and easier to make. The fascination of seeing a puri puff up as it is fried is quite unique, and there is nothing to compare with eating fresh warm puris.

MAKES 16–18 PURIS

225g (8oz) medium-grade chapaty flour   oil

1. Mix the flour with 1 tablespoon oil and enough warm water to make a firm dough. Knead the dough well, until it is smooth and elastic enough to pull without breaking.

2. Prepare 16–18 small balls, each about 2.5cm (1 inch) across, and roll each one out to a 6cm (2½ inch) disc.

3. Heat the oil in a deep frying pan, a wok or a karahi and deep-fry the puris. Depending on the size of the pan, you can fry 3–4 puris together. The puri will puff up into a ball and float on the surface. When it does this, turn it over until it is brown on both sides (about 1 minute on each side). Lift it out and place it on kitchen paper to draw off the excess oil.

4. Serve the puris hot or cold, taking care not to squash them.

· SWEET PURIS ·

This is a typical Gujarati dish (known as dhebra), in which jaggery is used to sweeten the puris. Serve them warm with Green Moong Bean Curry (p. 62) or cold with chutneys and relishes. They keep well for 2–3 days, so they are good to take on picnics.

MAKES 42 SWEET PURIS

2 tablespoons jaggery or brown sugar   oil
175g (6oz) chapaty flour

1. Dissolve the jaggery or brown sugar in 7 tablespoons hot water (sieve the liquid to remove the grit that often sticks to jaggery).

2. Mix the flour with 1 tablespoon oil and most of the sweet water to make a soft dough. Knead for 3–4 minutes until smooth and divide the dough into 7 equal-sized balls.

3. Use a little oil on the rolling surface and roll each ball of dough out to a disc approximately 15cm (6 inches) in diameter. Use a sharp knife to cut each disc into 6 triangles or wedges.

4. Heat the oil in a deep frying pan and fry the sweet puris until golden on both sides.

5. Serve hot or cold.

· MASALA PURIS ·

These puris are quick to prepare and good to eat with any spicy curry or just as a snack with tea or coffee.

MAKES 16–20 PURIS

225g (8oz) medium-grade chapaty flour
1 teaspoon salt
1 teaspoon chilli powder

½ teaspoon ground turmeric
oil

1. Mix the flour with the salt, chilli powder, turmeric, 1 tablespoon oil, and enough water to make a soft dough, either by hand or using a food processor.

2. Knead the dough well until it is smooth and elastic enough to pull without breaking.

3. Break off a 2.5cm (1 inch) piece, roll out to an 8cm (3 inch) disc and place on greaseproof paper. Repeat with the rest of the dough. Or you could roll a bigger piece of dough into a big circle and cut small circles from it using a round pastry cutter.

4. Heat the oil in a deep frying pan and drop in the puri, 2–3 at a time, very carefully. If the oil is at the right temperature, the puri will immediately puff up into a ball and float on the surface. When it does this, turn it over, until it is crisp and golden on both sides. Lift it out and place it on kitchen paper to draw off the excess oil.

5. Eat the puris hot or cold.

· CORNMEAL PURIS ·

These spicy cornmeal puris (known as vada) keep well for many days. Eat them with a curry, with plain yogurt or as a quick snack with tea.

MAKES 15 CORNMEAL PURIS

5 tablespoons coarse cornmeal
1 tablespoon gram flour
1 tablespoon chapaty flour
1 tablespoon finely chopped fresh or
   dried fenugreek leaves
1 tablespoon fresh coriander leaves,
   finely chopped
1 teaspoon finely chopped green chilli
1 teaspoon salt

1 teaspoon roasted cumin powder
1 teaspoon sugar
1 teaspoon lemon juice
1 teaspoon sesame seeds
¼ teaspoon ground turmeric
½ teaspoon baking powder
1 tablespoon oil
2 tablespoons yogurt
extra oil for frying

1. Put all the ingredients, except the extra oil, into a bowl. Add 1–2 tablespoons water and mix by hand to make a soft dough. Let it rest for 20 minutes.

2. When ready to cook, grease your hands with a little oil and make the dough into 15 small round balls. Place 4–5 balls of dough between 2 pieces of greaseproof paper or muslin cloth and use the back of a wide spoon to press them into 5cm (2 inch) wide puris.

3. Heat some oil in a wok or deep frying pan. Gently lift each puri and deep-fry (4–5 puris together, depending on the size of the pan). When golden on one side, turn over and cook on the other side. Some of the puris will puff up.

4. Serve hot or cold.

· NAAN ·

Ready-made naan is easily available now from supermarkets, but there is nothing like a fresh, hot, home-made naan covered with melted butter, nuts and coriander. This recipe is simplicity itself.

———————————— MAKES 10 NAAN ————————————

225g (8oz) self-raising flour
1 × 6g (⅛ oz) sachet easy-blend dried
  yeast
½ teaspoon salt
2 tablespoons natural yogurt
1 tablespoon oil

4 tablespoons warm milk or water
a little butter (optional)
a few flaked almonds (optional)
a few fresh coriander leaves (optional)

1. Mix the flour, yeast, salt, yogurt and oil with enough warm milk or water to make a soft dough. Cover and let it rest in a warm place for 25 minutes.

2. When you are ready to make the naan, knead the dough for 2–4 minutes until it is smooth. Then take a small ball of dough, the size of a golf ball, and roll it out to the shape of a small pitta bread. Repeat until you have about 10 naan.

3. Cook them under a hot grill for about 2 minutes on each side, until they puff up like balloons.

4. Brush the naan with a little butter, garnish them with almonds and coriander leaves if you wish, and serve.

· BHATURA ·

Bhatura is another very popular bread. Made from self-raising flour, it puffs up when fried like a puri. Occasionally, I add 1 tablespoon fenugreek leaves to the recipe. The green speckles look attractive and give the bhatura a mild bitter taste.

Bhatura are usually served with Spicy Chickpeas and Spinach (p. 66); in India the dish is called Chana Bhatura. Left-over bhatura, lightly grilled, taste excellent with Coriander Chutney (p. 92), Green Chillies Stuffed with Peanut Masala (p. 98) and Stir-Fry Relish (p. 96).

MAKES 10–12 BHATURA

175g (6oz) self-raising flour
1 dessertspoon oil
1 tablespoon yogurt

½ teaspoon salt
extra oil for frying

1. Mix all the ingredients, except the extra oil, in a bowl. Add 2–3 tablespoons water to prepare a soft dough. Let it rest for 15 minutes.

2. Knead the dough well for 2–3 minutes until it is no longer sticky, then divide into 3cm (1½ inch) balls. Use a thin rolling pin to roll each dough ball out to a thin 8cm (3 inch) round.

3. Heat some oil in a wok or a deep frying pan. Gently lift each bhatura and deep-fry 2–3 together (depending on the size of the pan). The bhatura will puff up and float on the surface. When they do this, turn them over until they are brown on both sides. Lift them out and drain on kitchen paper.

· STUFFED PARATHAS ·

Paratha is a flat bread, similar to chapaty. It is cooked on an oiled griddle or frying pan. Plain parathas make a good accompaniment for any curry. Just follow the method below, but ignore the stuffing. They can be prepared early and then be warmed under a grill or wrapped in aluminium foil and placed in a warm oven.

This traditional potato-stuffed paratha is excellent as a simple lunch dish, served with Cucumber Raita (p. 102).

——— MAKES 8 PARATHAS ———

PARATHAS
225g (8oz) chapaty flour
1 teaspoon salt
1 tablespoon oil
extra oil for frying

STUFFING
2–3 potatoes, peeled and boiled
2 teaspoons oil

½ teaspoon mustard seeds
½ teaspoon cumin seeds
1 green chilli, finely chopped
1 tablespoon finely chopped fresh
    coriander
½ teaspoon salt
½ teaspoon chilli powder
a little sugar
lemon juice to taste

1. Prepare the parathas by mixing the flour, salt and oil with enough warm water to make a stiff dough. Knead for 2–4 minutes until it is smooth and does not stick to your hands.

2. To make the stuffing, mash the boiled potatoes. Heat the oil in a pan and add the mustard and cumin seeds. Let the seeds splutter; then add the mashed potato, green chilli, coriander, salt, chilli powder, sugar and lemon juice. Cook the stuffing for 5 minutes. Divide this mixture into 8 equal-sized balls; lightly oil your hands if the mixture is sticky.

3. To roll a paratha, take a 5cm (2 inch) ball of dough, roll it a little, place a ball of stuffing in the middle, gather the dough around the stuffing into a ball again, and gently roll it out to a 10cm (4 inch) wide paratha. Use a little extra flour to assist in rolling. Repeat until you have about 8 parathas.

4. Sauté each paratha for 2 minutes on each side over a medium heat on a griddle or in a frying pan. Spread 1 teaspoon oil around each paratha as it cooks on one side, then spread another teaspoon oil around as it cooks on the other side. Cook until brown on both sides.

—— VARIATION ——

Mooli (a long white radish available in some supermarkets and Asian shops) also makes an excellent stuffing for parathas. Eat these with Avocado and Tomato Raita (p. 103) or Red Pepper Chutney (p. 94).

—— MAKES 8 PARATHAS ——

1 white mooli
salt (to taste)
1 green chilli, finely chopped
1 tablespoon finely chopped fresh
   coriander

½ teaspoon chilli powder
½ teaspoon roasted cumin powder (p. 8)
Oil for frying

✦ Make the paratha dough as opposite.

✦ Finely grate the mooli, mix it with salt and let it rest for 5–7 minutes.

✦ Squeeze out all the liquid. Add the fresh chilli, coriander, chilli powder and cumin powder. Mix well and divide the stuffing into about 8 balls.

✦ Roll and stuff the parathas as opposite, and sauté for 2 minutes on each side over a medium heat on a griddle or in a frying pan. Spread 1 teaspoon oil around each side of the paratha as it cooks, until brown on both sides.

· MASALA ROTLAS ·

Millet, which is the main ingredient of this bread, is the most popular grain in India next to rice and wheat. It has more protein, vitamin E and iron than wheat. However, when making millet rotla, a little wheat flour is added so that it is easier to digest, and the combination of the flours improves the protein content. You can get millet flour from most Indian grocers; store it in the fridge or freezer to keep it fresh.

Rotlas can be prepared early and served hot or cold. They are excellent with natural yogurt.

MAKES 5 ROTLAS

6 tablespoons millet flour
2 tablespoons chapaty flour
2 tablespoons gram flour
1 teaspoon chopped green chilli
1 teaspoon grated fresh ginger
3 tablespoons natural yogurt
2 tablespoons oil
a handful of chopped fresh or dried
   fenugreek leaves
a handful of chopped fresh coriander

1 teaspoon jaggery or brown sugar
   (optional)
1½ teaspoons salt
1 teaspoon chilli powder
½ teaspoon roasted cumin powder (p. 8)
½ teaspoon ajwain seeds
1 teaspoon lemon juice
a pinch of ground turmeric
1 teaspoon sesame seeds
extra oil for frying

1. Put all the ingredients, except the extra oil, into a bowl. Mix by hand to make a stiff dough, using 1 tablespoon water if required. Knead for 3–5 minutes.

2. Divide the dough into 5 balls, each about 5cm (2 inches) across. Take one of the dough balls, place it between 2 plastic freezer bags or 2 sheets of cling film and, using a thin rolling pin, roll gently on top of the plastic to form a big flat rotla, about 10cm/4 inches across. Repeat until you have 5 rotlas.

3. Place the rotla on a griddle or in a heavy frying pan, spread 1 teaspoon of oil around it and cook over a medium heat for 1 minute. Turn over, spread another teaspoon of oil around the rotla and cook for a further 2 minutes. Turn over again and cook for another 2 minutes. It should be brown on both sides.

CHAPTER SEVEN

CHUTNEYS, RELISHES & DIPS

Often, just a teaspoon of chutney or a relish is all that is needed to give character to a plain dish. They are great accompaniments to any meal, be it simple or complex.

Most chutneys and relishes can be kept in the fridge for a few days, and it's worth freezing Coriander Chutney and Tamarind Sauce, as they are included in many recipes.

The Spicy Tomato Chutney, Yogurt and Onion Chutney, and Apple and Mango chutney can all be used as tasty dips for vegetable crudités, making refreshing and unusual starters.

Vegans can enjoy all the recipes in this chapter apart from those containing yogurt, which are Hot-Hot Red Garlic Chutney, Yogurt and Onion Chutney, Mooli Relish, Mogri Relish and Avocado and Tomato Raita.

OPPOSITE PAGE 90: Gram Flour Pancakes (page 21), Spicy Tomato Chutney (page 94), Spiced Sprouting Bean Salad (page 68)

OPPOSITE, TOP TO BOTTOM OF PLATE: Cluster Bean Curry (page 51), Potato and Stuffed Baby Aubergine Curry (page 45)

· CORIANDER CHUTNEY ·

This chutney freezes very well so it's worth making a double or quadruple quantity and freezing the extra in plastic ice cube trays. When the cubes are solid, remove them from the ice trays and store in a plastic box in the freezer. These coriander cubes are indispensable; you can stir them into lentil curries and rice dishes at the last minute for a wild dash of colour and taste.

Both the leaves and the stalk of the coriander can be used for this chutney. You only need to remove the root base of the stalk.

½ bunch fresh coriander, chopped
3–4 long green cayenne chillies
a 2.5cm (1 inch) piece fresh ginger,
   peeled and cut into chunks
6–8 peanuts

a little sugar
salt (to taste)
½ teaspoon roasted cumin powder (p. 8)
1–2 teaspoons lemon juice

1. Put all the ingredients in a food processor, together with 2 tablespoons water (or more, if you prefer a thinner green chutney). Blend to a smooth paste.

—— VARIATION ——

If you have some fresh mint handy, you can add 2 tablespoons chopped mint to the above ingredients for a sparkling **Mint Chutney** – a superb addition to yogurt.

· TAMARIND SAUCE ·

Tamarind is a fruit which is sold in slabs as a dry paste including the seeds and fibres of the pod. It has a rich, fruity taste, and is used as a souring agent.

My recipe for tamarind sauce uses equal quantities of tamarind and seedless dates; or, alternatively, you can use a sweetener like jaggery or brown sugar.

Since it freezes well, it is useful to make a large quantity of tamarind sauce and freeze the extra in plastic ice cube trays. When the cubes are solid, remove them from the ice trays and store in a plastic box in the freezer.

—————— MAKES 450ml (15fl oz) SAUCE ——————

100g (4oz) block of tamarind	salt (to taste)
100g (4oz) seedless dates, jaggery or	a little roasted cumin powder (p. 8)
brown sugar	a little chilli powder

1. Put the tamarind and dates or jaggery or brown sugar in a pan. Add 600ml (1 pint) water, bring to the boil, and simmer for 10 minutes. Remove from the heat.

2. When cold, mix well and strain the juice through a sieve.

3. Season the sauce with the salt, cumin powder and chilli powder.

—— VARIATION ——

Alternatively, you can use a microwave oven. Soak the tamarind and seedless dates or jaggery or brown sugar in water for 20 minutes.

✦ Then microwave the mixture for 10–15 minutes, and strain the juice.

✦ Season to taste with the salt, cumin powder and chilli powder.

· SPICY TOMATO CHUTNEY ·

This versatile tomato chutney is ideal with all fritters or as a dip for Puris (p. 82) and Parathas (p. 88). It keeps well for 1–2 days in the fridge.

SERVES 2–4

2 big fresh tomatoes, skinned (p. 4)
2 teaspoons tomato purée (optional)
1 shallot or small onion, peeled
¼ green pepper, de-seeded
1 red or green chilli, de-seeded
a 2.5cm (1 inch) piece of cucumber

a 2.5cm (1 inch) piece of carrot
1 teaspoon salt
1 teaspoon vinegar or lemon juice
½ teaspoon roasted cumin powder (p. 8)
½ teaspoon chilli powder

1. Put all the ingredients together in a food processor. (If the tomatoes are very ripe, do not add the tomato purée.) Blend for 3–4 minutes, until everything is finely chopped.

· RED PEPPER CHUTNEY ·

One of my favourite chutneys; serve it with fritters or as a dip. It keeps well for 3–4 days in the fridge or you can make extra and freeze it in ice cube trays.

2 long red cayenne chillies, de-seeded
½ red pepper, de-seeded
½ teaspoon salt
½ teaspoon chilli powder

1 teaspoon lemon juice
10 cashew nuts
10 peanuts

1. Put all the ingredients in a food processor and blend to a smooth paste.

· HOT-HOT RED GARLIC CHUTNEY ·

This is absolute favourite to accompany Indian flat breads like Masala Rotlas (p. 90). It is for people who love garlic and hot food, and it keeps well in an air-tight container in the fridge for 4–6 weeks.

10–12 garlic cloves, peeled
2 teaspoons chilli powder
1 teaspoon salt

2 teaspoons oil
1 tablespoon lemon or lime juice

1. Put all the ingredients in a food processor and blend to a smooth paste.

· MINT & YOGURT DIP ·

This is the easiest dip and it keeps well in the fridge for a few days. Serve it with pappadums or Potato Fritters (p. 31).

SERVES 2–3

4–6 tablespoons Greek yogurt
2 teaspoons bottled garden mint sauce
  or 2 teaspoons finely chopped fresh
  mint

½ teaspoon salt

1. Mix all the ingredients together in a bowl and serve.

· YOGURT & ONION CHUTNEY ·

This mild-flavoured yogurt chutney is sensational with Fenugreek Fritters (p. 23) or you can serve it with any of the rice dishes.

───── SERVES 2–3 ─────

2 teaspoons oil
1 teaspoon husked urad dal, washed well
6–8 curry leaves
½ teaspoon asafoetida

1 small onion, sliced
1 teaspoon salt (or less to taste)
½ teaspoon chilli powder
4–6 tablespoons natural yogurt

1. Heat the oil in a small saucepan. Add the urad dal, curry leaves and asafoetida. Stir for 1 minute.

2. Add the sliced onion and stir-fry for 4–5 minutes. Add the salt and chilli powder; mix well and leave to cool.

3. Mix in the yogurt and serve.

· STIR-FRY RELISH ·

This is a very quick relish, nutritious and colourful. It can be served hot or cold but it *must* be eaten on the same day.

───── SERVES 4–6 ─────

1½ tablespoons oil
½ teaspoons mustard seeds
100g (4oz) white cabbage, shredded
1 carrot, cut into matchsticks
1 long green chilli, de-seeded and quartered lengthways

1 small green mango (optional), skinned and sliced into matchsticks
salt (to taste)
½ teaspoon sugar
½ teaspoon chilli powder
lemon juice (to taste)

1. Heat the oil in a wok or a large frying pan and add the mustard seeds and vegetables. Stir-fry for a few minutes.

2. Add the salt, sugar, chilli powder and lemon juice, and stir-fry for 4–5 minutes. Serve hot or cold.

· CAULIFLOWER RELISH ·

This is an unusual relish using crunchy cauliflower, tempered with mustard-flavoured oil. Serve it as part of a main meal, warm or cold, and it is better to eat it on the same day. It makes a delicious light lunch when served with Cucumber Raita (p. 102) and bread.

SERVES 4–6

1 small cauliflower
1 onion, peeled
1–2 green chillies, de-seeded
2 tablespoons oil

2 teaspoons mustard seeds
½ teaspoon asafoetida
1 teaspoon salt
lemon juice (to taste)

1. Cut the cauliflower into small bite-size pieces, about 2.5cm (1 inch) cubes. Chop the onion and green chillies into small pieces.

2. Heat the oil in a wok or frying pan and add the mustard seeds and asafoetida. As the seeds pop, add the cauliflower, onion and chilli.

3. Toss everything together for 3–5 minutes, just long enough to mix it but still keep the cauliflower crunchy.

4. Remove from the heat, and season to taste with salt and lemon juice.

GREEN CHILLIES STUFFED WITH
· PEANUT MASALA ·

In this exotic recipe, peanuts and gram flour are used to stuff Kenyan chillies; (for a milder taste, you can use small green peppers).

———————— SERVES 3–4 ————————

2 tablespoons oil
1 tablespoon gram flour
1 tablespoon chopped peanuts (ground in a coffee grinder)
1 teaspoon salt
1 tablespoon dhana jeera (p. 8)

¼ teaspoon ground turmeric
1 teaspoon lemon juice
4 Kenyan chillies
1 teaspoon mustard seeds
¼ teaspoon asafoetida

1. Heat 1 tablespoon oil in a wok over a medium heat, stir in the gram flour and cook for 3 minutes, until the flour changes colour to a light brown.

2. Add the chopped peanuts and cook for 2 more minutes, then add the salt, dhana jeera, turmeric and lemon juice. Mix well and stir-fry for 2 minutes.

3. Cut each chilli in half lengthways, scoop out the seeds and arrange the chillies in a serving dish. Use a teaspoon to stuff each half chilli with the peanut filling.

4. To the same wok (do not wash it), add the remaining tablespoon oil. When it's hot, add the mustard seeds and asafoetida. When the seeds pop, pour this flavoured oil over the stuffed chillies.

5. Serve cold.

· APPLE & MANGO CHUTNEY ·

This combination makes a very tasty chutney; use it as a dip or chutney for Potato Fritters (p. 31) or Fenugreek Fritters (p. 23). If you use a cooking apple, add a little more jaggery or brown sugar.

½ green dessert apple, peeled and roughly chopped
½ green unripe mango, peeled, stoned and roughly chopped

½ teaspoon salt
½ teaspoon chilli powder
1 teaspoon jaggery or brown sugar

1. Put all the ingredients in a food processor, together with 2 tablespoons water (or a little more if necessary). Blend to a purée and serve.

· APPLE RELISH ·

Here, cooking apple is stir-fried in mustard-flavoured oil to make a tasty accompaniment to any dish.

2 teaspoons oil
1 teaspoon mustard seeds
½ big green cooking apple, peeled and cut into big chunks

½ teaspoon salt
½ teaspoon chilli powder
1 teaspoon sugar

1. Heat the oil in a small pan and add the mustard seeds. When the seeds splutter, add the apple pieces, and stir-fry for 2–3 minutes.

2. Add the salt, chilli and sugar, and cook for a few minutes till the apple is soft. Serve hot or cold.

· RED ONION RELISH ·

Spiced raw red onion complements many curries. Try it with Stir-Fried Okra (p. 42), Potato and Cauliflower Curry (p. 39) and Green Pepper and Tomato Curry (p. 56).

1 red onion, peeled and finely chopped	¼ teaspoon chilli powder
¼ teaspoon salt	a squeeze of lemon juice

1. Mix all the ingredients together in a bowl and leave to infuse for 20 minutes before serving.

· MOOLI RELISH ·

The long, white mooli radishes sold in some supermarkets and Asian and Chinese grocers are full of protein, carbohydrate, calcium, phosphorus and iron. You can eat them raw in salads, or sprinkle them with a little salt and chilli powder.

In many shops they sell thin, small, 15cm (6 inch) long white mooli with the greens still attached. Their taste is very similar to that of rocket leaves and they can be served in mixed salads.

My personal preference is to lightly stir-fry finely chopped mooli and mooli greens in spiced oil. (If you grow your own small, red-skinned radishes, do not uproot the radish bulbs. Eventually, when the small green seed pods grow, they can be chopped and stir-fried in the same way.)

SERVES 3–4

1 bunch of mooli (4–5 mooli) and mooli greens	salt (to taste)
	black pepper (to taste)
2 teaspoons oil	a little chilli powder
½ teaspoon mustard seeds	natural yogurt
½ teaspoon fennel seeds	

1. Grate the mooli and finely chop the greens.

2. Heat the oil in a wok or frying pan and add the mustard and fennel seeds. As the seeds start to pop, add the mooli and greens and stir-fry for a few minutes.

3. Season with salt, pepper and chilli powder, mix with an equal quantity of yogurt, and serve cold.

· MOGRI RELISH ·

At certain times of the year, you can get very long, pinkish-purple tender radish pods called mogri (these are the seed pods of the long white mooli). This delicate vegetable can be stir-fried in the same way as above.

───────────── **SERVES 3–4** ─────────────

1 bunch of mogri (10–12 mogri)	1 teaspoon dhana jeera (p. 8)
2 teaspoons oil	salt (to taste)
½ teaspoon mustard seeds	lemon juice (to taste)
½ teaspoon chilli powder	natural yogurt

1. Chop the mogri.

2. Heat the oil in a wok or deep frying pan and add the mustard seeds. As the seeds start to pop, add the mogri, chilli powder and dhana jeera. Stir-fry for a few minutes.

3. Season to taste with salt and lemon juice, mix with an equal quantity of yogurt, and serve cold.

· CUCUMBER RAITA ·

This quick and easy yogurt mixture has become a 'must' with any curry meal. In fact I love to serve it with any of my starters, or on its own – it is so cooling and refreshing.

SERVES 3–4

a 5cm (2 inch) piece of cucumber
1 small green chilli, de-seeded and finely
   chopped
1 tablespoon chopped fresh coriander
6 tablespoons natural yogurt
salt (to taste)

½ teaspoon roasted cumin powder (p. 8)
½ teaspoon mustard powder
½ teaspoon sugar
a few chopped fresh mint leaves

1. Chop or finely shred the cucumber and squeeze out most of the liquid.

2. Put the cucumber, chilli and coriander in a bowl with the yogurt, and mix well. Add the salt, cumin powder, mustard powder and sugar, and mix again.

3. Garnish with the fresh mint, and chill before serving.

VARIATION

You can also make **Fruit Raita** by adding chopped banana and tomato to the above mixture.

· AVOCADO AND TOMATO RAITA ·

Avocado raita is a new innovation.

SERVES 3–4

1 avocado
1 tomato, skinned (p. 4) and chopped
½ green chilli, de-seeded and chopped
1 shallot or 2 spring onions, finely
  chopped

1 tablespoon finely chopped fresh
  coriander
1 teaspoon salt
freshly ground black pepper (to taste)
6 tablespoons yogurt
½ teaspoon chilli powder

1. Cut the avocado in half, keeping the shell intact. Gently scoop out the avocado flesh and cut into small cubes.

2. Mix all the ingredients except the chilli powder together in a bowl and season to taste.

3. Serve, garnished with the chilli powder, in the avocado shells or a bowl.

CHAPTER EIGHT

SWEETS & DRINKS

Aɴ Iɴᴅɪᴀɴ ᴍᴇᴀʟ is not complete without a sweet, particularly at religious festivals, weddings or celebrations. A sweet is always offered to God to ask for blessings, before being eaten by the family – a ritual still followed on all auspicious occasions.

I have chosen some traditional sweets like Gulab Jambu and some sweets which are eaten with the main meal, such as Saffron-Flavoured Shrikand and Sweet Vermicelli. Some are my own creations, like Cashew Nut and Paneer Barfi, and there are some light, refreshing sweets to end a hot spicy meal, such as Mango Kulfi and Avocado Fool.

A popular ending to a hot curry meal is a medley of tropical fruits, served with fresh cream, ice-cream or Greek yogurt. My own favourite is Fruity Yogurt. To a bowl of Greek yogurt, simply add a little sugar and salt to taste. Then decorate with pineapple and walnut pieces. Alternatively, you can add red berries when they are in season.

The chapter ends with a selection of drinks.

· KHEER ·

Kheer is very similar to rice pudding, but this Gujarati version is laced with the delicate fragrance of saffron, cardamom and nutmeg and decorated with slivers of almond and pistachio nuts – a delicious dessert.

My personal favourite is cold kheer decorated with fresh cherries, mango or tangerines. (An unusual combination but it really works.)

SERVES 4

50g (2oz) pudding rice
600ml (1 pint) milk
2–3 tablespoons sugar
6–8 saffron strands
6 cardamom pods, slit open and seeds crushed

½ teaspoon freshly grated nutmeg
25g (1oz) slivered almonds
25g (1oz) pistachio nuts, chopped
2 tablespoons single cream or vanilla ice-cream (optional)

1. Wash the rice and place in a large pan. Add 250ml (9fl oz) boiling water and boil for 5 minutes.

2. Add the milk, bring back to the boil and lower the heat. Simmer for 20 minutes, until the mixture is thick and creamy.

3. Stir in the sugar and cook for 10 more minutes. Add the saffron, cardamom, nutmeg, almonds and pistachio nuts, and stir again.

4. Serve hot or cold, adding single cream or vanilla ice-cream if you wish, just before serving.

· SAFFRON-FLAVOURED SHRIKAND ·

A well known and popular sweet. Silky-soft, cold shrikand, flavoured with saffron, makes the perfect end to a meal on a hot summer's day. You can make it early, as it keeps well in the fridge.

The traditional method of separating the whey from the yogurt is to tie the yogurt in a cheese cloth and hang it for 3–4 hours. However, a much quicker and easier method is to put the yogurt in a cheese cloth bag, place several layers of newspaper on a table, put the cheese cloth bag containing the yogurt on top, cover with several more layers of newspaper, and place a weight on top. The whey will separate very quickly and will be absorbed by the newspaper.

SERVES 2–3

425g (15oz) low fat natural set yogurt
2 tablespoons sugar
½ teaspoon ground cardamom

6–8 saffron strands
chopped pistachios or slivered almonds

1. Separate the whey from the yogurt using the quick method described in the recipe introduction. This quantity of yogurt takes less than 20 minutes to separate and will produce about 4 tablespoons yogurt solids.

2. Put the yogurt solids, sugar and cardamom in a bowl and mix well for a few minutes, to get a smooth shrikand. (Always use 2 parts yogurt solids to 1 part sugar.) Spread the saffron strands on top, cover and refrigerate until ready to eat. The saffron will slowly seep through the shrikand, giving a beautiful colour and fragrance.

3. Decorate with pistachios or almonds before serving.

· CARROT HALWA ·

Carrot halwa is a traditional dessert, popular for festive occasions and wedding meals. To reduce the sweetness a little, you can serve it hot with vanilla ice-cream or cold with single cream. It keeps in the fridge for 4–5 days and freezes well.

SERVES 6–8

450g (1lb) carrots, peeled
1 tablespoon ghee or butter
a handful of whole skinned almonds,
    pistachio nuts and cashew nuts
4 whole cardamom pods

300ml (10fl oz) milk
100g (4oz) sugar
1 teaspoon rosewater (optional)
6–8 saffron strands

1. Shred the carrots finely in a food processor or with a hand grater.

2. In a large saucepan, melt the ghee or butter and add the almonds, pistachios, cashew nuts and cardamom pods. Stir for 1 minute.

3. Add the shredded carrots and stir-fry for 10 minutes over a medium heat, until the carrots have softened and cooked. Add the milk and cook for 10 more minutes, stirring 2–3 times.

4. Add the sugar and cook for a further 10 minutes, making sure that the mixture does not stick to the saucepan. Mix everything very well. The halwa should now be ready – thick and glossy. Add the rosewater and saffron for fragrance and serve hot or cold.

· SEMOLINA HALWA ·

This semolina halwa is simple, easy and tasty; a favourite for religious festivals.

SERVES 6–8

100g (4oz) sugar
50g (2oz) butter or ghee
100g (4oz) coarse semolina
6–8 saffron strands

½ teaspoon ground cardamom
1 tablespoon sultanas
1 tablespoon mixed chopped almonds
   and pistachio nuts

---

1. Put the sugar in a saucepan with 600ml (1 pint) water. Bring to the boil, and boil for 3–4 minutes until the sugar dissolves.

2. Melt the butter or ghee in a wok or frying pan, and add the semolina. Cook for 6 minutes, until the semolina mixture changes colour to a golden brown.

3. Add the sugared water and cook for about 20 minutes, until the halwa is soft and all the water has been absorbed.

4. Mix well, add the saffron strands, ground cardamom and sultanas and cook for a further 5 minutes. Place the halwa in a serving bowl and decorate with the chopped almonds and pistachios. Serve hot or cold.

· SWEET VERMICELLI ·

This is a very popular traditional sweet, known as beeranj in India. It is very easy to make and can be served hot or cold as part of a main meal with the hot curries.

SERVES 6

50g (2oz) butter or ghee
100g (4oz) dried vermicelli (fine thread-
   like pasta)
300ml (10fl oz) cold milk

150g (5oz) white sugar
10 almonds, finely slivered
seeds from 5 cardamom pods, crushed
6–10 saffron strands

---

1. Melt the butter or ghee in a big saucepan, break the strands of vermicelli and add to the saucepan. Stir-fry for 4–5 minutes, until the vermicelli is brown.

2. Mix the milk with 300ml (10fl oz) water and pour it gently into the saucepan, taking care not to splash. Mix well and let the mixture boil for a further 10 minutes.

3. Add the sugar, lower the temperature to a medium heat, cover and cook until the vermicelli is soft and most of the liquid is absorbed (about 15 minutes). At this stage a little butter or ghee will float on top.

4. Stir in the almonds, cardamom and saffron strands, and serve.

· AVOCADO FOOL ·

My passion for avocado is reflected in this light, tropical fruit fool, my own invention. The pale green colour of avocado and pistachio nuts, topped with kiwi or passion fruit, is most refreshing after a hot, spicy meal. This dessert is my son's favourite.

SERVES 4–6

2 ripe avocados, skinned and stoned
½ banana, peeled
4 slices fresh or tinned pineapple
175g (6oz) single cream

a little sugar (to taste)
75g (3oz) whole pistachio nuts
2 sliced kiwi fruit or the seeds of
  2 passion fruit

1. Put the avocado, banana, pineapple, cream and sugar in a blender or food processor and blend to a smooth purée. Add the pistachio nuts and mix well.

2. Decorate with slices of kiwi fruit or spread the passion fruit seeds on top. Cover with clingfilm and chill well. Try to prepare this dessert no more than 1–2 hours before the meal in order to prevent the avocado discolouring. You can of course serve it straight away if you have used chilled ingredients.

· GULAB JAMBU ·

Gulab jambu is a traditional sweet, made from milk which is boiled until it has a thick consistency (khoya).

This quick version uses powdered milk combined with fresh milk, the end result being just as good. The semolina balls are soaked in sugar syrup which is flavoured with rosewater. In the summer months, you can add fresh rose petals as a garnish (gulab means rose). Gulab jambu keeps well in the fridge for a few days.

SERVES 6

225g (8oz) sugar
6–8 saffron strands
1 teaspoon rose essence or 2 teaspoons rosewater
6 tablespoons powdered milk
1 tablespoon self-raising flour

1 tablespoon semolina
¼ teaspoon bicarbonate of soda
½ teaspoon ground cardamom
50ml (2fl oz) cold milk
extra oil for frying

1. First prepare a thin sugar syrup. Put the sugar in a pan with 900ml (1½ pints) boiling water, and boil until nearly half the water has evaporated. Add the saffron and rose essence or rosewater and keep the syrup warm.

2. Put all the remaining ingredients, except the extra oil, in a bowl and mix well. Use the milk to bind the mixture and knead gently until it forms a big soft ball and no longer sticks to your hands. Divide into 20 small balls and roll each one smoothly.

3. Heat the oil in a wok or deep frying pan and deep-fry the balls over a medium heat until golden. All the balls will rise to the surface while frying. Stir the oil with a wooden spoon so that they fry evenly and slowly puff up. Drain on kitchen paper to remove excess oil.

4. When all the balls are cooked, gently lower them into the sugar syrup, switch off the heat and cover the pan. The balls will get soft as the syrup seeps in. They can be eaten straight away, or they can be served later, warm or cold, in individual bowls with a little sugar syrup (reheat gently for warm jambu).

· Cashew Nut & Paneer Barfi ·

One day, while experimenting with my favourite ingredient, paneer, I ended up with this fudge-like sweet for which home-made paneer must be used. Serve these after a hot curry or with coffee. They keep well in the fridge for a week.

―――――――――― **Makes 25 Pieces** ――――――――――

175g (6oz) cashew nuts
175g (6oz) sugar
75ml (3fl oz) milk
1 teaspoon ghee or butter
1 teaspoon ground cardamom
6–8 saffron strands
12–15 pistachio nuts, halved (optional)

PANEER
1.2 litres (2 pints) milk
2 tablespoons natural yogurt
2–3 teaspoons bottled lemon juice

1. To prepare the paneer, boil the milk in a heavy-based pan. At boiling point, add the yogurt and lemon juice and stir until the milk starts to curdle. Strain the mixture through a large, fine sieve and use the milk solids (paneer) which will be approximately 175g (6oz). You can save the cooking liquid (whey) and use it as cooking stock (store it in the fridge for 2 days).

2. Grind the cashew nuts finely in a food processor.

3. Put the sugar and milk in a big pan and bring to the boil. Add the ghee or butter (this keeps the syrup shiny) and let it bubble for 5 minutes till it is thick and milky.

4. Add the paneer to the milky mixture and cook and stir over a medium heat for 5 minutes. Add the cashew nuts and ground cardamom and mix well. Stir for about 5 minutes, until the mixture no longer sticks to the pan.

5. Remove from the heat and spread the mixture on a lightly greased tray to a thickness of about 2.5cm (1 inch). Press the saffron strands on top and cut into 2.5cm (1 inch) cubes.

6. Decorate each barfi with half a pistachio nut placed in the middle.

· SAFFRON PEARLS ·

This is my prize-winning recipe, which I created in 1987 for a Diwali (festival of light) sweet competition, based on a simple idea of covering whole pistachio nuts or cashew nuts with a cooked almond paste and decorating them with saffron and cardamom. They look very tempting, they are easy to prepare and can be cooked early as they keep well. Serve them after a curry or with coffee.

MAKES 10–14 SAFFRON PEARLS

100g (4oz) whole blanched almonds or ground almonds
50ml (2fl oz) milk
50g (2oz) sugar
1 teaspoon ghee

10–14 whole pistachios or cashew nuts
6–8 saffron strands
½ teaspoon cardamom seeds, crushed or ground in a coffee grinder

1. If using whole almonds, grind them to a fine powder in a food processor.

2. Put the milk, sugar and ghee in a heavy-based pan, bring to the boil and let it boil for 5 minutes. Lower the heat to medium, add the ground almonds, stir and cook for a few minutes until the mixture forms into a ball. Stop cooking and let it cool.

3. When the mixture is cool enough to handle, divide it into 10–14 balls. Take a pistachio or cashew nut and mould the almond mixture around it. Shape it well. Repeat until you have 10–14 almond pearls.

4. Put the saffron strands in a saucer with a few drops of water. On top of each almond pearl, make a small dent and place a little cardamom powder and a drop of saffron water in it, with the undissolved strands. This will give it a festive look.

· MANGO KULFI ·

The taste of this home-made mango ice-cream is divine. I cannot find the right word to describe it but I am sure my Indian friends will understand when I say it is 'Amrut'. Serve this kulfi with slices of fresh mango if desired.

— MAKES 12 KULFI —

2 fresh ripe mangoes or 1 × 400g (14oz) can mango slices
900ml (1½ pints) milk

1 × 400g (14oz) can sweet condensed milk
4 tablespoons powdered milk
1 tablespoon chopped almonds or pistachio nuts

1. If using fresh mangoes, skin them, stone them and scoop out the flesh. If using tinned mangoes, drain the slices and discard the syrup.

2. In a jug, blend the milk, condensed milk, powdered milk and mango using a hand blender. Alternatively, use a food processor or liquidiser to blend until smooth.

3. Freeze the mixture in special aluminium conical kulfi moulds available from Indian shops. Decorate one end of the kulfi with the chopped nuts before freezing. The above quantity is enough for 12 kulfi containers. If you don't have kulfi containers, you can use ice cube trays. Allow 2–3 cubes per person.

· LASSI ·

Lᴀssɪ ɪs ᴍᴀᴅᴇ from equal quantities of natural yogurt and water – mixed with a whisk or by using an electrical mixer. It is either sweet or salted.

— VARIATIONS —

Salted Lassi

✦ Add a pinch of salt and decorate with roasted cumin powder (page 8) and mint leaves.

Sweet Lassi

✦ Sweeten to taste with sugar.

Mango Lassi

✦ Mix together equal quantities of natural yogurt, water and fresh or tinned mango juice. Add sugar to taste and mix well, until it is all frothy on top. Serve in tall glasses with crushed ice.

· FRESH MINT WATER ·

This mint water is a refreshing appetiser. Serve it in tall glasses, filled with a lot of crushed ice and garnished with a few fresh mint leaves. It keeps well in the fridge for a few days.

— MAKES 1.2 LITRES (2 PINTS) —

100g (4oz) fresh mint
2 tablespoons lemon juice or 1
  tablespoon Tamarind Sauce (p. 93)
1 teaspoon grated fresh ginger

1 teaspoon roasted cumin powder (p. 8)
½ teaspoon garam masala (p. 9)
2 teaspoons sugar
a few extra fresh mint leaves

1. Liquidise all the ingredients, except the extra mint leaves, with 1.2 litres (2 pints) water, and strain the glossy green liquid through a very fine sieve.

2. Store it in the fridge until ready to drink and serve garnished with a few fresh mint leaves.

· INDIAN MASALA TEA ·

Indian tea is brewed by boiling milk, water, tea leaves and sometimes sugar together. This spiced Indian tea is excellent for the throat; an ideal drink for the cold winter months. For special occasions, fresh grated ginger and saffron are added.

For 2 cups of Indian tea you need 400ml (14fl oz) water, 125ml (4fl oz) milk, 2–3 teaspoons tea leaves and sugar to taste. Mix in a pan, bring to the boil, stir a little and simmer for 7–9 minutes. Strain and serve.

To prepare masala tea, you need to add the following spice mixture while brewing the tea.

50g (2oz) ground ginger	25g (1oz) cinnamon sticks
50g (2oz) cloves	25g (1oz) cardamom seeds
50g (2oz) black peppercorns	

1. Mix all the spices together and grind to a fine powder in a coffee grinder. Store in a sealed jar.

2. Use ¼ teaspoon of this masala per cup and increase the quantity as you develop a taste for it.

· FRESH MANGO JUICE WITH GINGER ·

When fresh ripe mangoes are available, the best drink to accompany a spicy meal is mango juice.

1. Skin the mangoes, stone them and scoop out the flesh. Mix with water (the quantity depending on the consistency of juice you prefer) and sugar to taste.

2. Blend in a liquidiser until smooth, and strain.

3. Serve with lots of crushed ice, in tall glasses, during the summer months. For extra bite, sprinkle some ground ginger on top.

· LEMON AND LIME JUICE ·

A refreshing drink, similar to home-made lemonade. Prepare it when good quality, thin-skinned limes are available.

———— MAKES 8 GLASSES ————

4 tablespoons sugar (or more to taste)	½ teaspoon salt
juice of 2 fresh lemons and 2 fresh limes	a few fresh mint leaves
(approximately 225ml (8fl oz) juice)	

1. Put the sugar in a pan with 225ml (8fl oz) water and bring to the boil. Let it boil for about 10 minutes, until it is a thick syrup. Take off the heat.

2. Strain the lemon and lime juice, add it to the sugar syrup and mix in the salt. When the syrup is cold, bottle it and store it in the fridge.

3. When ready to serve, put 2 tablespoons syrup in each cocktail glass, fill with 125ml (4fl oz) cold water, add crushed ice and stir well. Decorate with fresh mint leaves and serve.

MENU SUGGESTIONS

THE MOST common request from students at my Indian cooking classes is for help in planning menus, so I hope the ideas and suggestions below will prove valuable.

Indian cuisine is infinitely rich and varied but most of us want to cook something quick and easy after work. For this reason, I've suggested a range of two-dish menus which are ideal for light meals. If you want a more substantial meal there are also some three-dish menus to choose from. Select your own combination of sweets and drinks from the recipes in Chapter Eight.

When entertaining, you may wish to prepare one or two extra dishes the day before (many can be refrigerated or frozen) and perhaps one or two quick chutneys and relishes. The only rule is to serve your food with imagination, so that it pleases the eye as well as the palate, the soul as well as the body.

TWO-DISH MENUS

Bhatura
Spicy Chickpeas and Spinach

*

Stuffed Parathas
Yogurt and Onion Chutney

*

Gram Flour Pancakes
Stir-Fry Relish

*

Masala Khichadi
Spiced Yogurt Soup

*

Spicy Puffed Rice
Cucumber Raita

Masala Rotlas
Hot-Hot Red Garlic Chutney

*

Paneer Tikka
Mint and Yogurt Dip

*

Naan
Mixed Dal with Fresh Spinach

*

Aubergine and Green Lentil Pullav
Avocado and Tomato Raita

*

Steamed Coriander Potatoes
Masala-Spiced Sugar Snap Peas and Cashew Nuts

Chana Dal
Boiled Rice

*

Stir-Fried Aubergine
Mooli Parathas

Quick Samosas
Spicy Tomato Chutney

*

Puris
Potato and Shallot Curry

THREE-DISH MENUS

Sweet Puris
Green Moong Bean Curry
Boiled Rice

*

Naan
Mattar Paneer
Cauliflower Relish

*

Saffron Rice
Yogurt Soup with Fenugreek
Dumplings
Gram Flour Pancakes

*

Coconut Soup
Creamy Mushroom Curry
Stuffed Parathas

*

Masala Puris
Potato and Cauliflower Curry
Yogurt Soup with Pasta Shells

Puris
Sweetcorn in a Spicy Peanut Sauce
Coriander Pullav

*

Cornmeal Puris
Potato and Green Pepper Curry
Apple Relish

*

Bhatura
Yellow Moong Bean Curry
Kheer

*

Naan
Paneer and Cashew Nut Korma
Stir-Fried Spinach or Spicy Potatoes
and Chickpeas

*

Bhatura
Potato and Stuffed Baby
Aubergine Curry
Sweet Vermicelli

IDEAS FOR PICNIC FOOD

Masala Puris
Spiced Rice Parathas
Sweet Puris
Cornmeal Puris
Cold Coriander Triangles
Gram Flour Pancakes
Potato and Shallot Curry (cold)
Paneer Tikka
Khandvi
Puff Pastry Samosas

Potato Fritters
Spicy Potato Balls
Spiced Sprouting
   Bean Salad
Cauliflower Relish
Coriander Chutney
Cucumber Raita
Gulab Jambu
Saffron Pearls
Onion Bhajis

IDEAS FOR BARBECUE FOOD

Vegetable Burgers
Cumin Cassava
Paneer Tikka
Chat Masala Salad

Cumin Potatoes
Sesame Potatoes
Stir-Fried Aubergine
Spiced Sprouting Bean Salad

SIMPLE FOOD
CLEAN MIND
HEALTHY BODY

INDEX

ajwain, 6
almonds: saffron pearls, 112
amchoor, 6
apples: apple and mango chutney, 99
    apple relish, 99
asafoetida, 7
aubergines: aubergine and green lentil pullav, 74
    potato and stuffed baby aubergine curry, 45
    stir-fried aubergine, 48
avocados: avocado and tomato raita, 103
    avocado fool, 109

bhajis, onion, 13
bhatura, 87
black-eye bean curry, 64
breads, 81–90
    bhatura, 87
    cornmeal puris, 85
    masala puris, 84
    masala rotlas, 90
    naan, 86
    puris, 82
    spiced rice parathas, 80
    stuffed parathas, 88–9
    sweet puris, 83
burgers, vegetable, 22–3

cardamom, 7
carrot halwa, 107
cashew nuts: cashew nut and paneer barfi, 111
    masala-spiced sugar snap peas and, 25
    paneer and cashew nut korma, 55
cassava, cumin, 15
cauliflower: potato and cauliflower curry, 39
chana dal, 61
chapaty, 82
chat masala, 7
chat masala salad, 26

cheese: hot toasted cheese and coriander sandwich, 20
    see also paneer
chickpeas: spicy chickpeas and spinach, 66
    spicy potatoes and chickpeas, 40
chillies, 2, 7
    green chillies stuffed with peanut masala, 98
    red pepper chutney, 94
chutneys, 91
    apple and mango, 99
    coriander, 92
    hot-hot red garlic, 95
    red pepper, 94
    spicy tomato, 94
    yogurt and onion, 96
cinnamon, 7
cloves, 8
cluster bean curry, 51
coconut, 2–3
    lemon rice, 72
coconut milk, 2
    coconut soup, 24
    potatoes in spicy coconut milk, 37
coriander, 8
    coriander pullav, 75
    hot toasted cheese and coriander sandwich, 20
    stir-fried potato and coriander, 30
coriander chutney, 3, 92
    cold coriander triangles, 17
    steamed coriander potatoes, 35
cornmeal puris, 85
cucumber raita, 102
cumin, 8
    cumin cassava, 15
    cumin potatoes, 28
curries: black-eye bean curry, 64
    cluster bean curry, 51
    creamy mushroom curry, 57

curried drumsticks, 52
green moong bean curry, 63
green pepper and tomato curry, 56
mattar paneer, 46–7
paneer and cashew nut korma, 55
potato and cauliflower curry, 39
potato and green pepper curry, 38
potato and shallot curry, 36
potato and stuffed baby aubergine curry, 45
sweetcorn and kidney bean curry, 67
yellow moong bean curry, 62

dal: chana dal, 61
mixed dal with fresh spinach, 65
deep-frying, 4
dhana jeera, 8
dips, 91
mint and yogurt, 95
drinks, 114–16
drumsticks, curried, 52
dry-roasting, 5
dumplings, fenugreek, 50

fennel, 8
fenugreek, 3, 8
fenugreek dumplings, 50
fenugreek fritters, 23
yogurt soup with fenugreek dumplings, 79
fool, avocado, 109
French bean curry, 51
fritters: potato, 31
fenugreek, 23
spinach, 23

garam masala, 9
garlic: hot-hot red garlic chutney, 95
red garlic potatoes, 34
ginger, 3, 9
fresh mango juice with ginger, 116
gram flour, 3
gram flour pancakes, 21
khandvi, 14–15
green moong bean curry, 63
gulab jambu, 110

halwa: carrot, 107
semolina, 108
herbs, 3
hot-hot red garlic chutney, 95

ice-cream: mango kulfi, 113
Indian masala tea, 115
ingredients, 2–4

karela, stuffed, 53–4
khandvi, 14–15

kheer, 105
kidney beans: sweetcorn and kidney bean
curry, 67

lassi, 114
lemon: lemon and lime juice, 116
lemon rice, 72
lentils: aubergine and green lentil pullav, 74
lime: lemon and lime juice, 116

mace, 9
mangoes: apple and mango chutney, 99
fresh mango juice with ginger, 116
mango kulfi, 113
mango lassi, 114
masala khichadi, 76
masala puris, 84
masala rotlas, 90
masala-spiced sugar snap peas and cashew nuts,
25
masala tea, 115
mattar paneer, 46–7
menus, 117–19
millet flour: masala rotlas, 90
mint: fresh mint water, 114
mint and yogurt dip, 95
mogari relish, 101
mooli: mooli relish, 100–1
stuffed parathas, 89
moong beans: green moong bean curry, 63
masala khichadi, 76
yellow moong bean curry, 62
mushroom curry, creamy, 57
mustard, 9

naan, 86
nutmeg, 9

oil, 3
okra: stir-fried okra, 42
stuffed okra, 43
onions: onion bhajis, 13
red onion relish, 100
yogurt and onion chutney, 96

pancakes, gram flour, 21
paneer: cashew nut and paneer barfi, 111
mattar paneer, 46–7
paneer and cashew nut korma, 55
paneer tikka, 12
pappadums, yogurt soup with, 80
parathas: spiced rice parathas, 80
stuffed parathas, 88–9
pasta shells, yogurt soup with, 80
pav bhaji masala, 10
pawa: spicy puffed rice, 73

peanuts, 4
  green chillies stuffed with peanut masala, 98
  sweetcorn in a spicy peanut sauce, 58
peas: peas in a spicy tomato sauce, 44
  stir-fried rice with peas, 77
peppers: green pepper and tomato curry, 56
  potato and green pepper curry, 38
potatoes, 27–40
  cumin potatoes, 28
  potato and cauliflower curry, 39
  potato and green pepper curry, 38
  potato and shallot curry, 36
  potato and stuffed baby aubergine curry, 45
  potato fritters, 31
  potatoes in spiced yogurt, 33
  potatoes in spicy coconut milk, 37
  quick samosas, 19–20
  red garlic potatoes, 34
  sesame potatoes, 29
  spicy potato balls, 32
  spicy potatoes and chickpeas, 40
  steamed coriander potatoes, 35
  stir-fried potato and coriander, 30
  stuffed parathas, 88–9
pullav (pullao): aubergine and green lentil
    pullav, 74
  coriander pullav, 75
pulses, 59–68
puris, 82
  cornmeal puris, 85
  masala puris, 84
  sweet puris, 83

raita: avocado and tomato raita, 103
  cucumber raita, 102
red pepper chutney, 94
relishes, 91
  apple, 99
  cauliflower, 97
  mogari, 101
  mooli, 100–1
  red onion, 100
  stir-fry, 96
rice, 69–78
  aubergine and green lentil pullav, 74
  boiled rice, 70
  coriander pullao, 75
  kheer, 105
  lemon rice, 72
  masala khichadi, 76
  saffron rice, 71
  spiced rice parathas, 80
  spicy puffed rice, 73
  stir-fried rice with peas, 77

rotlas, masala, 90

saffron, 10
  saffron-flavoured shrikand, 106
  saffron pearls, 112
  saffron rice, 71
salads: chat masala salad, 26
  spiced sprouting bean salad, 68
samosas, quick, 18–19
sandwich, hot toasted cheese and coriander, 20
sauce, tamarind, 4, 93
semolina halwa, 108
sesame potatoes, 29
shallots: potato and shallot curry, 36
shrikand, saffron-flavoured, 106
soups: coconut soup, 24
  spiced yogurt soup, 78–9
spices, 6–10
spinach: mixed dal with fresh spinach, 65
  spicy chickpeas and spinach, 66
  spinach fritters, 23
  stir-fried spinach, 49
sprouting bean salad, spiced, 68
sugar snap peas, masala-spiced cashew nuts and,
  25
sweetcorn: spicy sweetcorn, 16
  sweetcorn and kidney bean curry, 67
  sweetcorn in a spicy peanut sauce, 58
sweets, 104–13

tamarind sauce, 4, 93
tea, Indian masala, 115
techniques, 4–5
tomatoes, 4
  avocado and tomato raita, 103
  green pepper and tomato curry, 56
  peas in a spicy tomato sauce, 44
  spicy tomato chutney, 94
turmeric, 10

vegetables, 41–58
  vegetable burgers, 22–3
vermicelli, sweet, 108–9

yellow moong bean curry, 62
yogurt: avocado and tomato raita, 103
  cucumber raita, 102
  lassi, 114
  mint and yogurt dip, 95
  potatoes in spiced yogurt, 33
  saffron-flavoured shrikand, 106
  spiced yogurt soup, 78–9
  yogurt and onion chutney, 96